PENTECOSTAL PACIFISM
The Origin, Development, and Rejection of Pacific Belief among the Pentecostals.

JAY BEAMAN

WIPF & STOCK · Eugene, Oregon

Wipf and Stock Publishers
199 W 8th Ave, Suite 3
Eugene, OR 97401

Pentecostal Pacifism
The Origin, Development, and Rejection of Pacific Belief among the Pentecostals
By Beaman, Jay
Copyright©1989 by Beaman, Jay
ISBN 13: 978-1-60608-873-9
Publication date 10/13/2009
Previously published by Center for Mennonite Brethren Studies, 1989

To my parents, Warren and Jean Beaman,
who gave me a Pentecostal faith,

To my in-laws, Bob and Ima Lyons,
whose home I shared while writing
the first draft to this book.

ACKNOWLEDGMENTS

This book began as an independent study and then became a thesis while I studied at North American Baptist Seminary in Sioux Falls, S.D., under the direction of Dr. Stephen Brachlow. I am indebted to him for his gentle encouragement of the project. Vicki Biggerstaff, research librarian at North American Baptist Seminary, was of immense assistance in locating sources. Wayne Warner, director of the Assemblies of God Archives in Springfield, Mo., was of special help to me in finding resources, especially from the *Pentecostal Evangel*. People at the Pentecostal Archives at Oral Robert's University, in Tulsa, Ok., gave me free access to numerous documents.

Several times, I have travelled to Zion, Il., to study John Alexander Dowie, and have received a great deal of assistance there. Lee Deming, director of the Zion Historical Society's Shiloh House, the pastoral staff at the Christian Catholic Church, and Gladys Richert have all shown me Christian hospitality while I conducted research in Zion.

Donald Dayton, professor at Northern Baptist Seminary, Lombard, Il., read my thesis and gave helpful critique. John Howard Yoder, University of Notre Dame, also gave helpful advice. Recently, Wes Prieb, Director of the Center For Mennonite Brethren Studies, provided editorial assistance. Stan Friesen, a local artist, kindly produced the original artwork for the cover. Don Ratzlaff, editor of the Christian Leader, read the manuscript and offered helpful editorial comments.

Marcella Mohn, my secretary at Tabor College, typed the initial draft for the book. Brenda Hamm set the type and layout for the book, numerous times. My wife, Rockie, has given a part of her self to this book. She has read and corrected too many versions to remember, and taught me something about writing in the process. I hope I can express my gratitude to these many important people who helped make this book a reality.

Jay Beaman

Pentecostals, Peacemaking, and Social Justice
SERIES PREFACE

Pentecostal and Charismatic Christians comprise approximately twenty-five percent of global Christianity (around 600 million of 2.4 billion). This remarkable development has occurred within just the last century and has been called the "pentecostalization" of Christianity. Pentecostals and Charismatics experience Christianity and the world in distinctive ways, and this series invites discovery and development of Pentecostal-Charismatic approaches to peacemaking and social justice.

The majority of early twentieth-century Pentecostal denominations were peace churches that encouraged conscientious objection. Denominations such as the Church of God in Christ and the Assemblies of God said "no" to Christian combatant participation in war, and some Pentecostals and Charismatics are exploring this history and working for a recovery and expansion of this witness. The peacemaking aspect of the series focuses on pacifism, war, just war tradition, just peacemaking, peacebuilding, conflict transformation, nonviolence, forgiveness, and other peacemaking-related themes and issues within Pentecostal-Charismatic traditions and from Pentecostal-Charismatic perspectives.

Series Preface

We launch the series with a twentieth-anniversary reprint of Jay Beaman's *Pentecostal Pacifism*—an appropriate look back to the generative years of the Pentecostal movement when many denominations believed that nonviolence was a hallmark of the gospel of Jesus Christ.

Some early Pentecostals also confronted the injustices of racism, sexism, and economic disparity. Others perpetuated the problems. Yet the Holy Spirit leads us now, as then, to confront injustice prophetically and work to redeem and restore. Pentecostal-Charismatic Christians around the world are working for justice in a myriad of ways. This aspect of the series focuses on gender, race, ethnicity, sexuality, economics, class, globalization, trade, poverty, health, consumerism, development, and other social justice related themes and issues within the Pentecostal-Charismatic tradition and from Pentecostal-Charismatic perspectives. We understand that peace and justice are not separate concerns but different ways of talking about and seeking *shalom*—God's salvation, justice, and peace.

Forthcoming volumes include both original work and publication of important historical resources, and we welcome contributions from theologians, biblical scholars, philosophers, ethicists, historians, social-scientists, pastors, activists, and practitioners of peacemaking and social justice. We especially welcome both scholarly and praxis-oriented contributions from majority world Pentecostals and Charismatics, for this series seeks to explore the ways that Pentecostal-Charismatic Christians can develop, strengthen, and sustain a peace-with-justice witness in the twenty-first century around the world. Royalties from sales of these volumes are often donated to Pentecostals & Charismatics for Peace & Justice (www.pcpj.org), a 501(c)3 network advocating for Jesus-shaped and Spirit-empowered peace with justice.

Paul Alexander, 2009

AUTHOR'S PREFACE
TO THE 2009 EDITION

If you have come to this volume for the first time without context, it surely must be bewildering. Perhaps you have been introduced to Pentecostalism in the public square with names like John Ashcroft and Sarah Palin or televangelists like Pat Robertson. They seem like the personification of the stereotyped religious right and what appears to be a blessing on blatant pursuit of empire. Who could forget John Ashcroft's folksy rendition of "Let the Eagle Soar." Is it possible that there is room in the same historical tent for ardent pacifists who believed they held the moral center for the movement?

I feel a bit like Rip Van Winkle, republishing a book that evoked a forgotten ethos, even twenty years ago when it was published by the Mennonites. In fact, it was written as a master's thesis twenty-seven years ago at North American Baptist Seminary in Sioux Falls, South Dakota. Christian pacifism was an issue that had sent me to seminary in the first place. My hope in the first writing was to elicit in the reader some of the shock I felt, growing up as a Pentecostal during the Vietnam War, only to find out later that the earliest Pentecostals took a stance to participation in war that was radical by the standards of the 1960s.

I was helped and influenced by writings on the subject by Donald Dayton and Lucille Sider Dayton and by Robert Mapes Anderson. Certainly they had highlighted the rough outlines of a story I would try to tell in more detail. As a seminary student with a family, I could barely afford one archival trip to Oral Roberts University Archives in Tulsa, Oklahoma and the Flower Heritage Archives at the Assemblies of God headquarters in Springfield, Missouri. I slept in my car for three nights while gathering documents. It was for me the trip of a lifetime. Who could sleep anyway!

Perhaps for all of us, there are narratives that capture our imagination and from which we draw inspiration our whole life. That has been true for me. But after twenty-seven years? In fact, much has happened since the first publication of this book. For one thing, Holiness and Pentecostal scholarship has proliferated, and not a few authors have treated the subject of the Pentecostals and war in the context of their writings. This book now has a context of rich scholarship that has included its subject in a larger conversation.

One of the things I wanted to do initially and could not do was to find out what Pentecostal individuals did when they had to comply with the requirements of universal selective service, the draft, and the requirements of their stated faith. This book laid out what Pentecostals said about war, primarily at the time of World War 1, but some since have suggested that an early prophetic minority spoke and acted more clearly and univocally than the rest could follow. It is hard to imagine otherwise.

More recently, I was encouraged by a group of Pentecostal and Charismatic social justice advocates, including Paul Alexander and the "PCPJ.org" folks to republish this volume. Dare I say that the book, *Pentecostal Pacifism*, was something of a sleeper-cell for many of these years? In Pentecostals and Charismatics for Peace and Justice, this book has taken on a life of its own. Perhaps in the process this group has given a living and emergent expression to something that was too easily written off as historical anachronism. But this group also includes scholars who are publishing and teaching in related areas in ways I could not imagine.

For me the interest of Paul Alexander and others has provided an occasion, over the last several years, of reassessing early Pentecostal Pacifism. I have tried to introduce that project in a new introduction in this volume, but I warn you it is preliminary. I hope to write a new volume soon which will allow a further treatment of Holiness and Pentecostal pacifism, detailing the actual practices of early day Pentecostals using draft registration records, WWI classification records, and prison and trial records of Pentecostals who tried to walk the fine line between the dictates of their government and the call of Spirit and the Kingdom of God. I hope then to be able to place this in the context of emergent scholarship on the subject.

When I began this latest project, I wondered whether one might even be able to find much evidence of the actual practice of pacifism in official sources. I have been gratified to find evidence that Pentecostal congregations and adherents took seriously the call from their leaders to promote peacemaking. For example, early day Pentecostals and Holiness folks went to jail for several things: for street preaching, for praying and preaching to loudly into the wee hours of the morning in the neighborhood, for praying and failing to take children to the doctor . . . but in World War I, they were imprisoned most of all for resisting the war effort. In fact during World War I, the derogatory term "Holy Roller," came to be associated in the mass media with pacifism and trouble with the government over the war effort. In most churches during World War I, the call would go out, "pray for the boys at the front." Pentecostals also had some of those men to pray for, but Pentecostals were distinguished from the mainstream by their call to "pray for the boys in prison."¹

Another emergent theme I am finding in my current study is the convergence of Radical Holiness groups and Pentecostals on the issue of pacifism. Pacifism may come to be seen as a marker for the distinctive radical Holiness ethos. The commonality gives us retrospective evidence that the Pentecostal movement was cut from the same cloth as the radical end of the Holiness movement. Holiness and Pentecostal adherents even sought each other out for fellowship in prison. Moreover, when you see early Pentecostal, Charles Fox Parham preaching pacifism in Zion, Illinois, documented in this volume, he was using an issue dear to the hearts of the Christian Catholic Church in Zion, a radical Holiness group, as a way of competing with and recruiting from that group. I am also finding evidence of religious conscientious objection to World War I much more consistently in the radical Holiness and Pentecostal groups than in the Holiness groups that had come to be more institutionalized by that time.

However, it is not only the scholarship on Pentecostal pacifism that is emergent. Even if we consider Pentecostalism to be institutionalized, the current reality is changing as well. Recently, more than a hundred thousand Christians have come to this country from the former Soviet Union, who are themselves Pentecostals. These immigrants wish to join with established Pentecostal denominations in this country. Apparently one difficulty in that potential merger is the fact that the recent immigrants perceive the standard form of Pentecostalism in this country as militaristic, while they, on the other hand, are Pentecostal Pacifists, and to their way of thinking, always have been so.²

---

1   Please indulge me these musings at the present and allow me to footnote in detail as I tell this story more fully in a later book.
2   Darrin J. Rodgers conversation, June 2009, Flower Pentecostal Heritage Center, Springfield, MO.

Perhaps the Spirit has brought us to a moment of renewed conversation which can be informed in part by the prophetic utterance of early day Pentecostals and the experiences of contemporary outsiders. It may sound at first like an unknown tongue ... but wait ...

Jay Beaman, 2009

INTRODUCTION TO THE 2009 EDITION

In World War I, a very small number of men were counted as religious objectors. A large proportion of these were drawn from the historic peace churches, especially the Mennonites, Amish, and Hutterites, with a good representation from the Quakers. Yet, a small new sect, the Pentecostals also represented themselves to each other and to the government as Pacifist to war on the basis of their interpretation of the Bible and their claims about the Gospel as they understood it "in the latter days." They believed that their calling was to love all people and give witness in all the world, by the power of the Spirit. Like their immediate predecessors in the holiness movement "radical holiness" could include pacifism to war.[1]

---

1   Dayton, Donald W.,. *Theological Roots of Pentecostalism,* p.43, 76, 78, traces radicalism in the Holiness Movement to John Wesley, and the antislavery movement, also, Dayton, "Piety and Radicalism: Ante-Bellum Social Evangelicalism in the U.S.," in Christian T. Collins Winn, *From the Margins: A Celebration of the Theological Work of Donald W. Dayton,* p.31-41,. Also, Dayton, Donald W. and Lucille Sider Dayton. "An Historical Survey of Attitudes Toward War and Peace Within the American Holiness Movement," in *Perfect Love and War: A Dialogue on Christian Holiness and the Issues of War and Peace,* Paul Hostetler, ed. R.G. Robbins, *A.J. Tomlinson: Plainfolk Modernist,* p. 162, 273, fairly champions the term "Radical Holiness," and connects it to pacifism. Randall J. Stephens, *The Fire Spreads: Holiness and Pentecostalism in the American South,* like Robbins, traces Radical Holiness to Northern Holi-

Early Pentecostal leaders, used a rhetoric which represented pretty much the whole movement as pacifist. Evidence for this can be found in most Pentecostal groups from around the time of World War One. Moreover, evidence can be found in most locations where Pentecostals were found at that time around the United States, especially in the South and Appalachia, and in European countries where Pentecostalism was evident. It is also apparent that when called to arms by their government, Pentecostals in large numbers attempted to respond to the state in ways that were informed by their unique emerging faith. We can see evidence of fairly extensive practice of pacifism by the early Pentecostals as well as the trouble it caused them with their government.

One group which I had no opportunity to study at length for my earlier publication, The Church of God, Cleveland, Tennessee, was perhaps emblematic of former Holiness churches who turned Pentecostal and added a third blessing to the second, resulting in a three-stage process of conversion. In 1917, the Church of God (Cleveland, Tennessee) adopted a position "against members going to war," seventh in a list of mostly prohibitions against drinking liquor, using tobacco, wearing gold jewelry, belonging to lodges, and swearing. The simple prohibition "against members going to war," complete with numerous scriptural citations was twenty ninth in a list of official Church of God "Teachings."[2] However, as early as 1915, A. J. Tomlinson had written an editorial in the Church of God Evangel about "The Present Situation." He noted that war normalized the very behaviors punishable in times of peace, suggesting, "If this is not vilainous [sic] then we are without expression."[3] Tomlinson de-

---

ness missionaries spreading the anti-slavery message and later Christian pacifist ideas in the South.
    2   *Church of God General Assembly Minutes*, 1917, p. 65, Nov. 1-6, 1917, see *Church of God General Assembly Minutes 1906-2002*, 2006 CD, Dixon Pentecostal Research Center, Cleveland, Tennessee.
    3   Church of God Evangel, March 6, 1915, p1.

scribed the numerous practical losses for families and homes, resulting "... poverty and starvation," but moved quickly to relate this to the work of Satan, through whom, "... Millions of souls are driven by the cruel war lash in to the slaughter-pens of Hell."[4] He criticized the progressives, who "... yesterday ... were boasting of their high state of civilization, holding their peace conferences and planning to step right into a state of millennial peacefulness; to-day they are plunged beneath the surface of a crimson sea and bathing themselves in the blood of uncivilized barbarism." His argument critiqued the powerful and educated and placed the solution in identifying with the poor. "While the multitudes of 'up-to-date' people are studying the war problems ... [it] is a good time for us to humble ourselves a little lower and go among the common people and work for the salvation of their souls."[5] For Tomlinson, the solution was in fighting another war, waged for God with the discipline and sacrifice of soldiers; a war to persuade others into salvation. He grieved that some sons of Church of God members had already joined in the wrong war, WWI, for patriotic reasons.[6] As the United States entered the War in 1917, Tomlinson moved pastorally to ready the Church of God to resist the one war and fight full-on in the other war. He painted the big picture in which war was a cosmic power, "The awful war devil is still slaying his millions."[7] He was clear about the role of members of the Church of God,

> If we are of the world so we can take part in the wars then we are not of His kingdom ... We cannot serve God and Mammon. Math. 6:24 ... No doubt many of our people are wondering what to do in case our country gets into war. Shall we enlist in the governmental service and fight for our rights? Can we shoulder a gun

---

4 Ibid.
5 Ibid.
6 "While the Wars Rage We Must Be on Our Battle Field," *COG Evangel*, July 8, 1916, p1.
7 "The Awful World War: The War in Which We are Engaged Is of Far More Importance, Ours is a Spiritual Warfare", *COG Evangel*, Feb. 24, 1917, p1.

and march out to the battle front and point our gun toward our enemy and fire into his ranks and send his soul to hell, when Jesus, our King, tells us to love our enemies? Math. 5:44[8]

If that had been too subtle, he counseled, "Many conscientious men have refused to carry guns under any circumstances. They felt it was contrary to the spirit of their Lord."[9] The decision was spiritual, "The war demon may try to persuade you that your first duty is to the stars and stripes, but this is a delusion. And you should never permit the spell that catches the world to get a hold on you."[10] Again he argued members to engage in the other war, "We are short of soldiers now. We have none to give up to fight in carnal wars."[11] Tomlinson was not being theoretical. His laborer-ministers were always torn between making a living and holding evangelistic meetings.

I hope our ministers and workers will not say in their hearts. I'll work at my trade this year and next year I will give my time to the service of the Lord. Your service is needed this year. The battle is on now.[12]

Tomlinson continued to use the *Church of God Evangel* to counsel and advocate for the young men in their opposition to the war with practical advice on how to register as a religious objector. The church paper carried numerous prayers for draftees and even those who went to prison during and after the war and the report of one church member who was killed by a local sheriff for resisting the draft.[13]

---

8   Ibid.
9   Ibid.
10   Ibid.
11   Ibid.
12   Ibid.
13   *COG Evangel*, Je. 9, 1917, p2; Je. 30, 1917, p2, Jul. 7, 1917, p3.; Jul. 13, 1918, p2; Aug. 4, 1917, p2-4; Aug. 25, 1917, p1; Sept. 28, 1918, p2; Oct. 20, 1917, p3; Nov. 10, 1917, p2, 4; Dec. 29, 1917, p4; Jan.5, 1918, p2; Jan. 28, 1918,

Tomlinson was steadfast in these concerns. Less than six weeks before the universal draft he gave practical advice to draftees. It was not the Church of God's role to dictate specific action, and if they were forced into the military they may not be able to successfully refuse all service, but surely they must not do more than noncombatant service as a medic or hospital worker or preaching while being clear they were not to carry guns.[14]

The Extent to which Pentecostals Practiced Pacifism in World War I

It is one thing to make the case that WWI Pentecostals presented themselves as pacifist, and taught their followers to observe pacifism, either thoroughgoing conscientious objection or conscientious objection followed by non-combatant service—if required. It is another thing to document that early Pentecostals practiced conscientious objection when called upon to register for the draft. Over 25 years ago when I began this project, it was nearly impossible to contemplate finding the draft registration records of early Pentecostals. Two main problems presented themselves: finding lists of Pentecostal men in order to search for what they did when called upon to register for the draft, and finding individual draft registration cards from microfilm rolls. Both tasks seemed impossible. Pentecostals found official membership lists to be the very mark of dead denominationalism which they intended to reform. Even now, most Pentecostal history is focused on great lead-

---

p1; Feb. 16, 1918, p2; Mar. 16, 1918, p3 Mar. 23, 1918, p2; Apr. 27, 1918, p4; Je. 29, 1918, p2; Jul. 13, 1918, p2; Jul. 20, 1918, p1, 4; Oct. 5, 1918, p4, Oct. 19, 1918, p3; Nov. 2, 1918, p4; Nov. 10, 1918, p 4, p3; Feb. 1, 1919, p2; Feb. 22, 1919, p4; Apr. 12, 1919, p4; May 24, 1919, p3, May 31, 1919; p2; Dec. 20, 1919, p3; Jan. 17, 1920, p2; Jul. 17, 1920, p2; Aug. 28, 1920, p2, Apr. 2, 1921, p3; May 13, 1922, p4, Oct. 21, 1922, p2, May 12, 1923, p3.
14   Ibid.

ers in the movement, mostly preachers and organizers of denominations. Moreover, even recent histories which do much to elucidate the worldview of early Pentecostals do not provide a great deal of help in creating a list of laymen. Finding lists of "laymen" is very problematic, even given the great archival resources across various Pentecostal denominations. Secondly, finding individual draft cards without a previous localized grouping in a particular draft board was nearly impossible. Even recently, Grant Wacker, in the context of arguing Pentecostals complete accommodation to the WWI draft, suggested,

> The pages of AOG periodicals carried requests after request for prayer for the spiritual and physical safety of mothers' sons fighting overseas. No one requested prayer for conscientious objectors. One can only assume that they were either too few to count or that editors screened out such requests, knowing how most readers would react.[15]

Yet two weeks after the citation of prayer requests for soldiers given by Wacker, the same Assemblies of God publication actually did just that, it counted a few conscientious objectors, asked prayer for them, and apparently did so without constituency reaction.

> Fort Riley, Kans.
> I am sending you my tithes. Six Dollars and Seventy cents, because they belong to God and I want you to send it where it is most needed. I am from Trenton, Mo., was drafted the 23rd of July, and I ask you to pray for us that are saved that God will keep us near unto Him, and that God will save souls. If ever there was a time that souls needed salvation, it is now, and there are thousands of souls here who would be lost if Jesus

---

15 Wacker, *Heaven Below*, p. 247, citing *Christian Evangel*, Oct. 5, 1918, p. 15.

would come now. There are three boys here that belong to the Assemblies of God. As I am a believer in the Apostolic Faith I am glad that God has given us a place where we don't have to take up arms. God is able to take us through. Pray for this place.
—Oscar Barle, Base Hospital, Fort Riley, Kans.[16]

The man appears to be Oscar Clinton Barley, a 28 year old farmer from Missouri who did not ask for exemption on his draft card but appears to have done so soon thereafter. Oscar Barle, gives evidence, along with three from the Assemblies of God of serving non-combatant in a base hospital.[17] Still, Wacker's assumption that the conscientious objectors were too few to count, was probably good advice. In fact, finding them is much like finding a needle in a haystack. While it may well turn out that those attempting to register as conscientious objectors were a recognizable part of Pentecostalism, they were a really microscopic part of the approximately 24 million who registered for the World War I draft[18]. Moreover, the reason thus far that they are too few to count, is more likely that the number of Pentecostal laymen found on any denominational lists are so few from the time of WWI.

Apparently, the U.S. government did not keep a list of all the conscientious objectors as such. Mennonite scholars have done the most to list men who were found in the various military camps, military detention camps, and prisons[19]. More recently, the Swarthmore College Peace Collection has created an online database of conscientious objectors to World War I.[20] In the meantime, internet re-

---

16   "Reports from the Field," *Christian Evangel*, Oct. 19, 1918, p. 14.
17   Draft Registration Card, Oscar Clinton Barley.
18   Keith, Jeanette, *Rich Man's War, Poor Man's Fight*, p. 57.
19   For example, Mininger, *Religious C.O.'s Imprisoned at the U.S. Disciplinary Barracks, Ft. Leavenworth, Kansas*, 1919. There are a many Pentecostals in this list.
20   Currently there are 2021 names with information on each, http://130.58.64.153/fmi/xsl/SCPC_COWW1_table.xsl.

sources have proliferated dramatically making it possible to search genealogical records online through such sites as Ancestry.com and others. Central to these sites is the extensive indexed list of World War I Draft Registrations. It occurred to me that the time had come to research such a list against known lists of World War I era Pentecostal males. Finding such lists has proved daunting.

The Pentecostal WWI Demographic Database

An iterative and emergent methodology was needed to construct lists of early Pentecostal males from the time of WWI. Two main lists have provided the backbone of my search, the list of ordained ministers and missionaries published in the General Council of the Assemblies of God from 1914 to 1924[21] and the list of officials including ministers (Overseers and Bishops), evangelists, deacons, and clerks of the Church of God (Cleveland, TN) from 1917 to 1925.[22] Along with both groups of names, states and cities were entered into a database. The Church of God records were supplemented with a photocopy of a hand-written list of early church members and a photocopy of a fund-raising list from an early auditorium in Cleveland, Tennessee. In 1915 and 1925 the Iowa State (Farm) Census asked a religious affiliation question. A modest number of Iowa Pentecostals from several groups were found in this way. From Sherry Sherrod DuPree's, *Biographical Dictionary of African-American, Holiness-Pentecostals 1880-1990*, I was able to find 76 names and demographics of males whose age at World War I was appropriate. Various Pentecostal

---

21   *Assemblies of God Publications Pre-WWII*, from the Flower Pentecostal Heritage Center at www.AGHeritage.org/shop.

22   David Roebuck, Director of the Hal Bernard Dixon Jr. Pentecostal Research Center, Cleveland, Tennessee, provided two extensive hand written photocopies of the first thirty pages of the Auditorium Receipts List from about 1914 and an early Church of God membership list. He also wisely suggested the CD, Church of God General Assembly Minutes 1906-2002.

Histories as well as newspaper accounts turned up a smaller number of names from that era. Mel Roebeck was kind enough to share a list of Azusa Street names, some of which I did not have and some who were young enough at Azusa to still be of draft age by World War I. Finally, the online list of religious objectors collected by the Swarthmore Peace Collection contributed at least twenty names identified as Pentecostal. The database has grown to 4,560 names with more added as they are made available.[23] In time, I envision the database to be a dynamic source of early Pentecostal demographic and biographical information.[24]

The database is biased towards available sources, and thus has 3,257 names associated with the Church of God (Cleveland, TN), 934 names from the Assemblies of God, and 146 names from a variety of other groups. One fourth of the names were female and three-fourths male. The male names were used to search for draft cards. Of 3,481 males, 1,558 (45%) of draft cards or census document were found. The 55% of Pentecostal male names not found fall into four overlapping groups: 1) those with common names found numerous times but with no clear way to distinguish which was the correct one, 2) those whose name had two initials and a last name and the two initials could signify many actual names, 3) those old enough that they didn't have to register for the draft, 4) those whose cards are simply not in the catalogued online database.

Draft cards were of three types, Type I from June 5, 1917, with a line to register exemptions, Type II from Sep-

---

23   Since doing this analysis and writing this paper, I have added 711 records from the Pentecostal Assemblies of the World, including 232 draft cards found thus far and 32 religious objectors found. With the help of David Daniels, I have also found 300 COGIC related names. This brings the database total to over 5,560. Since these recent records are not cleaned or analyzed they are not in the counts or analysis yet. In a forthcoming work, I will analyze these and other records I am working on obtaining presently.

24   I hope in time to be able to publish the database and publish something more about the social class and other demographic analysis of early Pentecostalism.

tember 12, 1918 without an exemption line, and Type III cards with little useful information. Only 681 Type I cards have been found thus far, from June 5, 1917, the earliest required registration, and the only type of card with an exemption request line. Type I cards are most crucial for examining religious objectors. Males between the ages 21 and 31 inclusive, were required to register on June 5, 1917. Thus, Type I cards are reflective of this age group, the prime group for the draft. Almost ten million men registered on June 5, 1917.[25] Type II, registration from September 12, 1918 yielded 815 cards. These cards did not give exemption status, but did give the name of the closest relative, usually the wife. A third type of card, with much less useful information, was found 33 times and census documents found about fifty times when a draft card could not be found. Of the 681 Type I cards and another nine cards with useful information, 252 or 37% of the Pentecostal draft registration cards where exemptions could be registered, were found to be religious objectors to World War I.

However, some of the religious objectors were registered in the draft as having the occupation of minister. When all draft cards with occupation of minister are selected out, we are left with 528 Type I cards, with the possibility of registering an exemption. Of the 528 Type I cards registering as "laymen," 165 or 31.3% asked for religious exemption. Thus, of non-ministerial Pentecostals, where the draft card allows us to know if they asked for exemption, almost one third asked for religious conscientious objector status. In the absence of better information, it also seems reasonable to assume that those Pentecostal men with Type II draft cards, without exemption status on the card, would have registered as COs in about the same proportion. Moreover, it seems reasonable to assume the same for Pentecostal men for whom we have not been able to identify their draft

---

25   *Report of the Provost Marshal General to the Secretary of War*, p. 24.

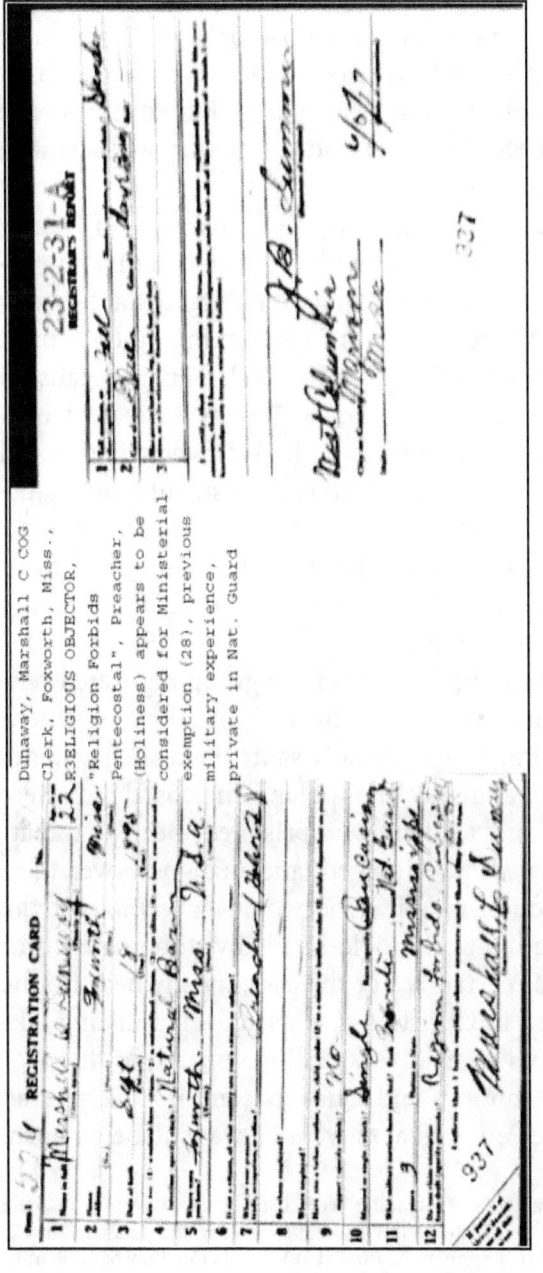

Type I Draft Registration Card. Notice line 12 for registering an exemption request. This image reprinted by permission of Ancestry.com. To view additional family history records, please visit www.ancestry.com. Annotation is mine.

cards. The assumption that about one third of Pentecostal men registered religious CO status to World War I, may be a conservative estimate, since we have evidence some number of Pentecostal men seemed to have assumed that God would protect them from being drafted and hence did not attempt to claim CO status until they were actually drafted.

Moreover, my database, The Pentecostal WWI Demographic Database, is created with the potential that numerous men in the database were not even Pentecostal converts until after WWI, even though I am looking up their draft registration status at the time of WWI. This is because, I included sources up to the year 1925 in my database, which allows for up to seven years after the War where men could have converted and been added to the list, but I am counting them as non-pacifist at WWI when they may not have been Pentecostal yet. Thus, the estimate of about one third of Pentecostal men attempting to register CO to WWI is probably very conservative.[26]

Even so, when over a third of the group registered religious conscientious objection during World War I and Pentecostal denominations officially sanctioned such a stand, this was overwhelmingly unpopular. Pentecostal men were killed, tarred and feathered, imprisoned, beaten, threatened, investigated, interrogated, and maligned over their religious objection to war. One would have thought the religious objectors were single-handedly stopping the war effort. That was certainly not the case, mostly because the number of men in Christian groups actively resisting taking up arms was so relatively small compared to the larger society. Mennonites and Quakers were relatively small groups and the Pentecostal movement was still being born.

---

26   The advantages of including Pentecostal list records up to 1925 are that 1) I had the potential to greatly expand the size of the database, and 2) young men who were laymen at the time of WWI or before they became ministers could be included in the database.

The societal reaction to religious conscientious objectors was more over the symbolic nature of their resistance and the potential it had for delegitimizing the righteousness of the war effort.

Pentecostal Religious Objectors in Context

In fact, overall, of almost ten million registrants on June 5, 1917, less than one third were called up and fifty percent of the draftees claimed some exemption.

> Of the claims made . . . 39 per cent of persons called, or 77.86 per cent of claims made, were granted . . . . 81.79 percent of claims made before local boards were granted.[27]

Thus, exemptions were widely, one could even say, routinely given. Of the 1.6 million exemptions given:

- 74% were for family dependency
- 20% were on the basis of being non-resident alien
- 6% were for occupation or vocation (including farming, strategic industries, and ministerial)
- 0.34% were for religious belief (3,887).[28]

Dependent Relatives Exemptions and Others

Nationwide, 48% of the 3.1 million men called up were married. Of these, 89% were given exemption to take care of family. Of all the exemptions, this must have seemed the most reasonable, fair, and culturally acceptable. Some draft boards "discharged all or virtually all married men."[29] Pentecostal registrants were also ready to ask for family exemptions. Of 681 Pentecostal men between the ages of

---

27 Report of the Provost Marshal General, p.24.
28 Ibid.
29 Ibid., p. 51.

21 to 31 registering on June 5, 1917, 37% were religious objectors, 23% registered requests for exemption based on family dependents, 5% requested both religious and family exemption, and 55% requested one or the other exemption. Fifty-seven percent of the 681 men were married and 27% of these were religious objectors, 35% requested family exemption, 5% requested both, and 53% requested one or the other exemption. Forty-three percent of the 681 men were single and 48% of these were religious objectors, 14% requested exemption to care for relatives (usually parents), 5% of single Pentecostals requested both religious and family exemptions, and 57% requested one or the other exemption.

The following table summarizes this data together with national rates.[30]

Requests for Family Dependent or Religious Exemption to WWI				
Exemption Request	National Registration	Pentecostals		
		Married 57%	Single 43%	All
Family Dependents	37.00%	35%	14%	23%
Religious Objectors	0.17%	27%	48%	37%
Both	—	5%	5%	5%
One or the other	37.17%	53%	57%	55%

Several things become apparent from this table. First, in the national population, the largest group of exemption requests, 37%, was for family dependents. Among Pentecostals it is the second largest reason for exemption, 23% overall and 35% among married men. However, the national rate of requests for religious exemption is 0.17%,

---

30   The national rates were calculated from *The Report of the Provost Marshal General* by taking the rates of family exemption and religious exemption granted, 74% and 0.34% respectively, times 50% of all men, the rate of men who requested exemption. The rates for Pentecostals are the actual rates requested in the sample.

and among the Pentecostals at 37%, and among single Pentecostals 48%. Taking the two kinds of exemption together, Pentecostals requested exemption at 55%, a great deal higher than the national rate of 37.17%. The rate for Pentecostals was fairly stable whether or not the registrant was married at around 55% requesting exemption. However, single Pentecostals, not having access to the family exemption as readily as married men, were almost twice as likely to register religious exemption over their married counterparts. This suggests that some Pentecostals who were not strictly religious objectors may have been able to satisfy both their religious affiliation and their government by taking the family exemption, if possible, and that they were not so ideologically driven as practical. It may well be that once the general direction of non-participation, where possible, in active pursuit of the war was enjoined, it was not so important how the goal was achieved. Of course, the family exemption was the largest exemption nationally, but not the only one. While 50% of the registrants nationally requested some exemption,[31] 399 or 59% of the 681 Pentecostals in the sample requested some exemption, significantly higher than the nation and for different reasons.

Denominations Represented among Pentecostal Religious Objectors

Of the 252 Pentecostal Religious Objectors to World War I Identified thus far, the largest group were from the Assemblies of God and the Church of God, Cleveland, Tennessee. The Assemblies of God were half of the group and Church of God, Cleveland, more than one fourth; together 75% of religious objectors I have found. Men from these two groups represented themselves using the two official names, Assemblies of God, or more formally, The General

---

31   Ibid., p.24.

Council of the Assemblies of God, and Church of God as well as other designations. Individuals I knew to be from both the Assemblies of God and Church of God on the basis of denominational sources were self-identified in the draft registration cards as Pentecostal, Pentecostal faith, Pentecostal church, Pentecostal sect, Apostolic faith, Apostolic Assemblies, Apostolic religion, Apostolic Holiness, or just plain Holiness. At the time of World War I, some still identified with an earlier denomination, such as Church of the Brethren or even Quaker. One self-identified as Methodist Episcopal. Those identified using records outside of the Assemblies of God and Church of God, Cleveland, were a smaller number and from a variety of groups including those mentioned above, as well as: the Pentecostal Assemblies of the World, Church of God in Christ, Church of God and Saints of Christ, and Church of the Living God. These draft cards are a testament to the widespread deep concern about the appropriateness of Pentecostals going to war. There is evidence that almost every Pentecostal group at the time of World War I encouraged conscientious objection and found some who heeded that call. Still, draft registrants from just about all Pentecostal groups could also be found in Type I draft cards, who left the exemption line blank or sometimes stated "none." Thus, the choice of religious exemption was not nearly universal among Pentecostals.

What form did the request for exemption, line 12 on the June 1917 Draft Card, take among Pentecostals?

One was not required to request exemption at the time of registering for the draft card to get an exemption, but certainly advised. The draft registrant was given up to two weeks to complete an exemption form with the local draft board. Thus far, I have not been able to find any of these exemption cards and have received feedback that they were probably destroyed after the war. Therefore, the cryptic one line short response on line 12 becomes one of the only windows into the experience of the registrant, and that only in the case of Type I cards.

Exemption Assumed, yet Unstated

There must have been numerous Pentecostal men who believed God would not let them be drafted and not until they were drafted did they ask for exemptions. They may not have wished to be confrontational, hoping they would not be drafted at all. There were examples of those who appear to have not requested an exemption on the draft registration card but were later found in conscientious objector barracks at a military camp. Edwin Mosses Bernhard, a 28 year old hat-presser, working in a factory in Reading, Pennsylvania, and apparently a member of the Assemblies of God, did not claim exemption at the time of filling out his registration, in June 1917, instead claiming conscientious objector status in October, 1917, probably sometime after being drafted. He was discharged for health reasons.[32] Thomas Martin Cain, a 23 year old single machinist and member of the Church of God (Cleveland, TN), from Knoxville, Tennessee, registered in the June 5, 1917 registration, answering "no" on the exemption line, but in August 1917 Cain had a letter intercepted by the U.S. Postal Authorities and used by the FBI to investigate the recipient, Fred L. Ryder, a Church of God Missionary to Argentina. According to Mickey Crews, Ryder's letter suggested he was pleased he went to Argentina in May 1917 before being drafted. Ryder was investigated throughout the War as

---

32   Swarthmore College Peace Collection online database. Mosses Bernhard, Draft Registration card.

a suspected draft evader. Cain had asked Ryder details on how to effectively avoid being drafted. Ryder pointed Cain to seek help from his denomination and its Executive, A. J. Tomlinson. For his part, Ryder stayed in Argentina for the duration, only returning to the U. S. in 1923.[33]

When, Hosea Brayles Roberts, a 23 year old single farmer, filled out his draft registration in June 1917, on the exemption line, instead of asking for an exemption, he stated "No Sir". But, in 1919 he was charged at Ft. Leavenworth with disloyalty and sentenced to 25 years in prison, with the sentence later reduced. Somewhere between the time he filled out his draft registration and finishing basic training, he decided he was a religious objector. No doubt, many Pentecostal young men had little clear instruction in how to register their religious objection.[34] The autonomy of local draft boards in carrying out registration must have also accentuated the difficulties, since there was probably little uniformity in instructing young men in the details of the registration process. Ora Lee, a Church of God, Cleveland, TN, member who did not request exemption later was found in Ft. Riley along with Mennonite war resisters.[35] But many young men must have seen the exemption line and the instructions given as suggestive that they would be given the exemption they requested, encouraging their listing an exemption.

Standard form Religious Objection

There were attempts to clarify, before the June 5, 1917 draft registration what would be the situation for religious objectors. About a week before registration day, newspa-

---

33 Crews, *The Church of God: A Social History*, p. 123. Draft Card, Thomas Martin Cain, June 5, 1917, Knoxville, TN.
34 Draft Card for Hosea Brayles Roberts. Swarthmore College Peace Collection online database.
35 Draft Card, Ora Lee

pers began carrying instructions from the government about how to file for exemption. The publications referenced question 12 which would ask, "Do you claim exemption from the draft? (specify grounds.)" In the case of religious objection prospective registrants would be told, "If you claim to be a member of a religious sect whose creed forbids its members to participate in war in any form simply name the sect."[36] The Government also made clear that groups which did not hold to pacifism before the draft would not be allowed to become pacifist after the draft. In its official publications the Assemblies of God, for example, published its position against going to war[37] and very brief instructions to young men on the process they would find at their draft boards. The June 2, 1917 *Weekly Evangel* warned all men ". . . age 21 to 36 inclusive—should be sure to register," and that there would be a place to register conscientious objection and the religious body that objected to taking human life of which one was a member.[38] It appears that the intention of the exemption line was that many men who belonged to groups that required religious objection to war would simply name their membership in that group specifically and that would be enough to signal the draft board to a pre-designated list of groups that fit the category. Thus, for example, one finds draft cards for Mennonites and Quakers, the most well known pacifist groups, to simply list the name of the group to which the registrant belonged.

In the same fashion, Pentecostals could and did simply list the group to which they belonged which disallowed participation in war. I have found at least six men who simply

---

36   "Draft Questions and How to Answer," *NY Times*, May 23, 1917, p.2.
37   "Resolution Concerning the Attitude of the General Council of the Assemblies of God Toward any Military Service which Involves the Actual Participation in the Destruction of Human Life," *Weekly Evangel*, Aug. 4, 1917, p.6.
38   "Concerning Registration for Military Service," *Weekly Evangel*, June 2, 1917, p.6.

listed "Pentecost" or "Pentecostal" as the affiliation which warranted exemption, and a similar group simply listing "Apostolic Faith" for exemption, much the same way that a couple of men simply listed "Holiness." This suggests the fact that these men saw no need to list a specific denomination, among the Pentecostal denominations, but that the movement as a whole was taken by these registrants to be pacifist. Still, among the Assemblies of God and Church of God (Cleveland, TN) registrants, numerous registrants simply put "Assemblies of God" or "Church of God" on the exemption line. About a fifth of the conscientious objectors found in the Assemblies of God and nearly half in the Church of God (Cleveland, TN) simply listed the name of the denomination.

Another sizable group of Pentecostal religious objectors simply put the locus of decision on membership in their church, which they did not name, as in "religious sect don't believe in war," or "against my church," or "my church don't believe in war," or "religious creed," or "Pentecostal convictions object to war", or "having membership of church that forbids taking of life." Scribal influence on the exemption line, given that some men couldn't write and others answered the questions orally, and the need for parsimony in a limited writing space dictated that the largest group of Pentecostal religious objectors simply made a cursory mention of "religion," "religious reasons," "religious views," "religious belief," "religious grounds," or "religious scruples." A smaller group appealed to conscience by name as in "conscientious objector," "conscientious scruples," "conscientious grounds," "conscience will not permit me to kill," "conscience will not permit me to take human life," and "conscience will not permit me to kill, even for the state." A similar appeal was in religious belief with a slight detail, "don't believe in war," "religious views opposed to war," "religious belief forbids killing fellow man," "religious belief…

against killing mankind," "scriptural," "Word of God," and "scripture and conscience against taking human life."

Two Pentecostals gave what would today be very unusual views; Bruno M. Berger a 23 year old single switch-board tester from Florida, simply listed "13th Amendment" the prohibition against slavery, and Arthur Mitchel Clark, a 22 year old Pentecostal farmer from Tennessee, simply stated "Nothing except don't want to go." The latter was still in the disciplinary barracks at Ft. Leavenworth in 1919 after the war ended, although records there indicated his reason for not wanting to go to war, was indeed religious.[39]

One twenty year old Assembly of God minister reflected theologically on his exemption entry in a way that simultaneously took advantage of his unusual name, Royal Bert Fields, writing, "Now expatriated through oath of allegiance to the Kingdom of God."[40] In this way, he attempted to make explicit on his draft card what some of the more cursory entries listed earlier may have only hinted. In doing so, Royal exemplified a potent underlying notion of the rule of God expressed in a decision which most young men of the time had become convinced they had no right to make. He felt his Pentecostal faith informed his decision to resist this most fundamental requirement of the state, expressed in the draft, calling upon an alternative allegiance to God's rule which freed him from the requirement to take a position of enemy against the people of another state.

Geographical Locus of Pentecostal Pacifism in the United States

Where did conscientious objectors identified as Pentecostal come from in World War I? In records examined thus far, they have been identified most with the South and

---

39 Swarthmore College Peace Collection online database.
40 Royal Bert Field, Draft Card.

to a lesser extent the Midwest. In some ways this is a reflection of the underlying sources of the lists which I used to search for their draft cards. For example, with the Church of God, Cleveland, Tennessee, the largest group I identified hailed from Tennessee. Many were found in Mississippi, Alabama, Florida, Georgia, North and South Carolina, West Virginia, Virginia, Missouri, and Arkansas. While it is not surprising that their locations reflected the initial reach of their various denominations, it is amazing to think of requesting conscientious objector status in World War I in the deep South and Appalachia.[41] Fully two-thirds of identified Pentecostal objectors came from the South, deep South, and Appalachia, followed by seventeen percent from the Midwest, eleven percent from the West and two percent from the Northeast. Pentecostal religious objectors were also found in at least 34 states.

Ethnic and Racial Groups

Like the early Pentecostal movement as a whole, Pentecostal objectors were also found among American minorities. Among 250 Pentecostal religious objectors identified primarily in draft cards, ten (4%) were African Americans and two were Hispanics (1%). African Americans may have found it difficult to register their conscientious objection with racist draft boards. In many cases, it appears the registrant did not actually write responses on the card, but answered questions to someone else who was filling out the card. Theodore Kornweibel documents the rumors that spread around the black Pentecostal denomination,

---

41   Keith, Jeanette, *Rich Man's War, Poor Man's Fight*, documents the social class origins of a particularly widespread resistance to the draft among rural, hill country, southerners. In her presentation, there were two southern responses to the WWI draft: 1) merchant class, wealthy class, and media supported the draft, and 2) the working, rural, poor largely resisted the draft. I will take up these themes as they apply to southern Pentecostals in detail in a forthcoming book.

The Church of God in Christ and the pacifist preaching of its founder, Charles H. Mason, especially in the Mississippi delta around Holmes County.[42] One newspaper rumored that the government had published a list of 70 blacks in Holmes County, who were evading the draft and offered a reward for their capture.[43] However, in an exhaustive search of over six thousand draft cards from Holmes County, only one obvious religious objector was found, George Gordon Allen, a single 22 year old farmer, and he was listed as white. Allen requested exemption saying, "Don't want to break 6th commandment."[44] A 37 year old Holmes County Preacher, from Lexington, Mississippi registered for the draft listing his occupation as Preacher, with the Sanctified Church. James Lewis Lee was probably able to get a ministerial exemption.[45] Lee was questioned by the Bureau of Investigation's agent in regard to his associations with C.H. Mason and the Church of God in Christ. Lee denied he or Mason ". . . preached antidraft or antiwar messages."[46] However, whether through connection to C.H. Mason and the Church of God in Christ, which taught pacifism, or through the Sanctified Church listed on his draft card, which insisted that "members should not take part in war,"[47] Lee was an African American Pastor associated with pacifism.

A black, 30 year old Pentecostal minister in the Pentecos-

---

42 Kornweibel, *"Investigate Everything,"* 2002, p. 149-162.
43 "Draft Evasion in Holmes County Due to Pro-German Teachings Among Blacks," *Vicksburg Evening Post*, Vicksburg, Mississippi, April 1, 1918, p.1.
44 George Gordon Allen, Draft Card, Durant, MS, but registered in Holmes County.
45 James Lewis Lee, Draft Card, Lexington, Holmes, MS.
46 Kornweibel, p. 154. After I found James Lewis Lee's draft card in a systematic search of Holmes County, MS, draft records, Kornweibel's book gave the connection to the Church of God in Christ and C.H. Mason, and Kornweibel documented the Bureau of Investigation's questioning Lee.
47 Piepkorn, p. 33. Whether it was the Christ's Sanctified Holy Church (West Columbia, South Carolina) or more likely the Christ's Sanctified Holy Church (Jennings, Louisiana) which came out if the former in 1903 is unclear.

Introduction

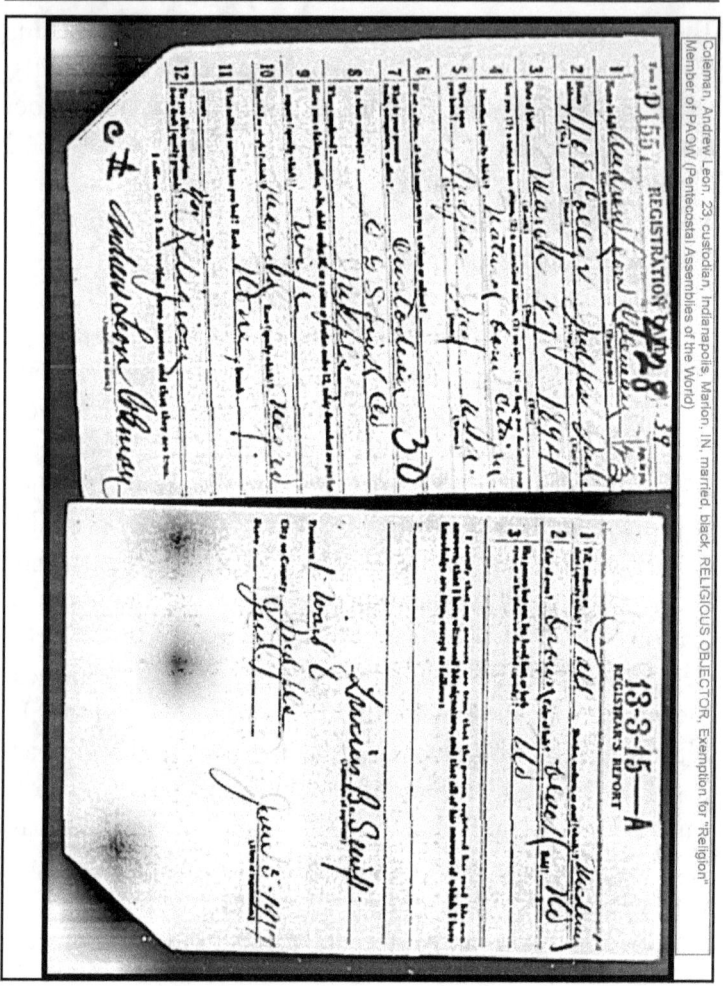

This image reprinted by permission of Ancestry.com. To view additional family history records, please visit www.ancestry.com. Annotation is mine.

tal Assemblies of the World, Joseph Marcel Turpin, from Baltimore, Maryland,[48] registered as a religious objector, and for exemption simply listed "Religious." His draft card gave his occupation as Minister of the Gospel, Apostolic Faith of Assembly.[49] He was more likely to have been exempted for being a minister than being a religious objector. Another Pentecostal Assemblies of the World Pastor, Elder Morton, "a well-known black pastor of Detroit and Windsor [Ontario]," was sentenced and served time in Kingston Penitentiary . . . for his conscientious objection to WWI.[50] William Henry Robinson, a 25 year old brick layer's helper from Toledo, Ohio and Andrew Leon Coleman, a 23 year old custodian from Indianapolis; were both members of the Pentecostal Assemblies of the World and requested religious objector status on their draft cards.

Robert Russell, a black, 27 year old laborer at the Transcontinental Compress Company listed "Religious Convictions," when requesting exemption.[51] However, the timing of his registration July 23, 1918, on a card designed for June 5, 1917, suggests a problem. In fact, June 14, 1917 he had been arraigned on charges of failure to register. At the time, he tried to make the case that he was a Pentecostal and believed that the command, "Thou shalt not kill," applied. When pressed further, he said he would obey God rather than man.[52] It appears that after a year in jail he was registered, asking for exemption as a religious objector. Russell's case further illustrates the possibility that more

---

48   Dupree, p. 275 gives a brief biographical annotation.
49   Joseph Mossell Turpin Draft Card, From the handwriting, it is obvious someone else filled out the card and he gave his signature. He signed Joseph Marcel Turpin.
50   Marilyn Stroud to Jay Beaman, email, Aug. 23, 2007. Marilyn Stroud is the Archivist for the Pentecostal Assemblies of the World Archives in Canada. She sent me extensive quotations from archival files created by former archivist and pastor, Douglas Rudd.
51   Robert Russell, Draft Card, July 23, 1918.
52   Stephens, p.261, "Holy Roller Held for Failure to Register," *Dallas Morning News*, June 15, 1917, p. 3.

Introduction

African-American Pentecostals may have opted out of registration altogether. In fact, Jeanette Keith suggests that in the South, a large proportion of blacks did not register, and if they did register and get drafted, they did not present themselves for service.[53]

Could Pentecostals be distinguished as Pacifists in WWI?

Was it a part of the public persona of Pentecostals in WWI that they were pacifists? The following example is taken from the government's attempt to show that the public including all religious groups were behind the war effort. In an attempt to motivate appropriate support of the Selective Service system, the government published lists such as the following to illustrate widespread church support for the war.

The following table summarizes a Jan., 1918 religious census of Camp Grant, in Rockford, Illinois.[54]

Camp Grant, IL. Religious Census, January 1918			
Agnostics	21	Mennonites	2
Apostolic	2	Methodists	3610
Armenians	1	Mission Friends	2
Atheists	13	Moravians	7
Baptists	1733	Mohammedans	2
Bethany	1	Mormans	72
Carmelites	1	New Church	1
Church of Christ [Union]	8	New Emmanuel	1
Church of God	1	New Thought	2

---

53 Keith, Rich Man's War. I plan to use this analysis in more detail in a forthcoming work to answer the question of why I have routinely found white Pentecostal's and seldom found black Pentecostal's draft registration cards.
54 "Camp Creeds," *Chicago Daily Tribune*, Jan. 22, 1918, p.7.

Church of the Nazarene	2		Orthodox	2
Christian Scientists	233		Pentecostal	3
Congregationalists	851		Plymouth Brethren	2
Disciples of Christ	522		Presbyterians	2188
Dunkards	9		Progressive	3
Episcopalians	1096		Quakers	45
Evangelical	107		Rationalists	4
Federated Church	1		Reformed	53
Free Mission	12		Roman Catholics	7678
Freethinkers	112		Saints of Christ	1
Golden Rule	2		Spiritualists	3
Greek Catholics	270		Swedish Mission	19
Holy Rollers	2		Theosophists	1
Infidels	1		Unitarians	120
Jews	658		United Brethren	78
Kriquorenes	1		Universalists	95
Lutherans	3943		Zionists	8
Total	**23605**			

Pentecostals can be found in this military camp, but in very small numbers. The "Apostolic" group here is probably a Mennonite-derived group found mainly in Illinois and Iowa, and not the "Apostolic Faith" Pentecostal group. Assembly of God is completely missing from this list, despite numerous Assemblies of God churches in Illinois and surrounding states. The one "Church of God" soldier could be one of several Holiness groups or the Pentecostal variety. Three "Pentecostal" and two "Holy Roller" adherents were found for a total of five who were clearly Pentecostal. Other groups known to be pacifist were found here as well; 2 Mennonite and 45 Quakers were found. It is possible that the Pentecostals, Quakers, Mennonites, and Apostolics were in fact conscientious objectors held in the military camp, or more likely that some of them were non-combatant soldiers, but they could have been combatants as well. Either way, five Pentecostals in this camp out of 23,605 in the census seems to suggest there were not so many Pentecostal soldiers.

Of course, the Pentecostal movement was small at the time, but these numbers are certainly more in line with what we would expect if the group maintained its pacifism in practice as well.

Moreover, not only were very few Pentecostals among the soldiers counted at Camp Grant, Illinois, conversely Pentecostals were also prominent among the religious objectors "on trial" at Camp Grant. The news stories sensationalized how "the board of inquiry on investigations of conscientious objectors arrived in camp and put army slackers through another grilling under orders from the Secretary of War Baker." The same reporter documented at length the cross-examination of a non-religious conscientious objector and briefly noted, "Other objectors represented the Moody Church, Russellites, Mennonites, Dunkards, Apostolites, Pentecostalites, and the Assembly of God."[55] Not only were the Assemblies of God not found among the soldiers at Camp Grant, the Assemblies of God and other Pentecostals were prominent among the religious objectors. Only the Moody Church, founded by D.L. Moody, himself a pacifist to the Civil War, stands out in this list as generally non-pacifist.[56] The rest were clearly pacifist

---

55   "Allison Faces Board; Pacifist Talk Cut Short," *Chicago Daily Tribune*, Jul. 3, 1918, p.7, ProQuest Historical Newspapers Chicago Tribune (1849-1986).

56   *Chicago Daily Tribune*, Jul. 3, 1918, p.7, ProQuest Historical Newspapers Chicago Tribune (1849-1986). A professor from Moody Bible Intitute in Chicago felt it necessary to point out that this lone religious objector did not in any way reflect on Moody Bible Institute, that the Moody Church and the Bible Institute were completely separate institutions, and that this professor had written a tract, justifying participation in war, for students to read.

churches. Finding Pentecostals classified in practice among the pacifist groups is completely consistent with their rhetoric at the time.[57]

Examination of the Pentecostal movement at the time of World War I, from the point of view of their beliefs, as represented by their rhetoric, shows widespread representation of the movement both to themselves and to the government as pacifist to war. This is true across the movement as measured by various denominational branches, or various places where Pentecostalism had taken hold by that time. More recently, it has become possible to examine the practice of World War I era Pentecostals, what they tried to do, in light of their rhetoric. What is now apparent is that not only was the belief fairly widespread among Pentecostals, but consistent with their overall style, when Pentecostals believed and preached something, they were not shy about attempting to practice the same. We can now find historical evidence of the practice of Pentecostal pacifism in World War I. This is all the more astounding when we reflect on the location of so much of the movement in the Deep South and Appalachia. Early Pentecostalism, in word and deed

---

57   It is possible to look in my data for Pentecostals in Illinois, the State in which Camp Grant was located. In The Pentecostal WWI Demographic Database, there are 115 persons from Illinois, 90 of whom were men, 47 of whom I found draft registration cards, and 25 of whom were of the age 21-31 in 1917 registration. Of the 25 Type I cards, eight chose no exemption, nine were religious objectors, seven requested family dependent exemption, and one requested ministerial exemption. In the June 30th edition of the *Weekly Evangel*, (p.8, "In Jail for Failure to Register") the editor told of receiving a letter from a Pentecostal woman in Anna, Illinois whose husband and brother-in-law were in jail for failure to register in the June 5th, 1917 registration. The editor of the Weekly Evangel chided the two men for very poor judgment, admonished them to repent of their mistake, and warned others to avoid their error. "If you have objections to slaying your fellow men, there is a time and place set apart for stating those objections, which will be heard and each case judged on its own merits. If there is good cause for exemption, exemption will be granted." In fact, two Assemblies of God men, from Union County, IL., John Fowler and Thurman Lee Harvick registered 20 days late, a punishable offense, and they registered as religious objectors. Did they fail to register? I am not certain these are the two in the article, nor that they ended up in Camp Grant pleading their case as religious objectors.

had much that could only be described as counter-cultural and even radical, according to some adherents, radical holiness. Early Pentecostals had stated beliefs which they used to clearly delineate their differences from the larger society in which they found themselves. Pacifism was only one way in which their beliefs must have made them seem unusual and even troublesome and at odds with the larger society. The practice of Pentecostal pacifism was especially tested, as were Pentecostals who had only recently officially articulated their pacifism, at the time of World War I.

Bibliography

Alexander, Paul. *Peace to War: Shifting Allegiances in the Assemblies of God.* Telford, PA: Cascadia, 2008.

"Allison Faces Board; Pacifist Talk Cut Short," *Chicago Daily Tribune, Jul. 3, 1918*, p.7, ProQuest Historical Newspapers Chicago Tribune (1849-1986).

Althouse, Peter. "Canadian Pentecostal Pacifism," *Eastern Journal of Practical Theology*, Vol. 4, 2, Fall 1990, p32-43

Assemblies of God Publications Pre-WWII, (2006) from the Flower Pentecostal Heritage Center at www.AGHeritage.org/shop.

Burgess, Stanley M. and Gary B. McGee. *Dictionary of Pentecostal and Charismatic Movements.* Grand Rapids, MI. Zondervan, 1988.

"Camp Creeds," *Chicago Daily Tribune*, Jan. 22, 1918, p.7.

Church of God General Assembly Minutes 1906-2002, CD, Cleveland: Tennessee, Dixon Pentecostal Research Center, (2006).

Church of God in Christ Yearbook. Memphis: Church of God in Christ Publishing House, 1951.

Crews, Mickey. *The Church of God: A Social History.* Knoxville: University of Tennessee Press, 1990.

Dayton, Donald W. *Theological Roots of Pentecostalism*, Metuchen: Scarecrow, 1987.

____. "Piety and Radicalism: Ante-Bellum Social Evangelicalism in the U.S.," in Christian T. Collins Winn, *From the Margins: A Celebration of the Theological Work of Donald W. Dayton*, p.31-41, Eugene, OR: Pickwick Publications, 2007.

Dayton, Donald W. and Lucille Sider Dayton. "An Historical Survey of Attitudes Toward War and Peace With the American Holiness Movement," in *Perfect Love and War: A Dialogue on Christian Holiness and the Issues of War and Peace*, Paul Hostetler, ed., Nappanee, IN: Evangel Press, 1974.

Dupree, Sherry Sherrod. *Biographical Dictionary of African-American, Holiness-Pentecostals 1880-1990*. Washington, DC: Mid Atlantic Regional Press, 1989.

"Holy Roller Held for Failure to Register," *Dallas Morning News*, June 15, 1917, p. 3.

Keith, Jeanette. *Rich Man's War, Poor Man's Fight: Race, Class, and Power in the Rural South during the First World War*, Chapel Hill, NC, University of North Carolina.

Kornweibel, Theodore, Jr. "Investigate Everything,": Federal Efforts to Compel Black Loyalty during World War I., Bloomington, IN: University of Indiana Press, 2002.

Marilyn Stroud to Jay Beaman, email, Aug. 23, 2007.

Robbins, R.G. *A.J. Tomlinson: Plainfolk Modernist*, New York: Oxford University Press, 2004

Stephens, Randall J. The Fire Spreads: Holiness and Pentecostalism in the American South. Cambridge, MA: Harvard University Press, 2008.

Swarthmore College Peace Collection online database of WWI Conscientious Objectors.

Tomlinson, A.J. "The Present Situation", *Church of God Evangel*, March 6, 1915, p.1.

____. "While the Wars Rage We Must Be on Our Battle Field", *Church of God Evangel*, July 8, 1916, p1.

____. "The Awful World War: The War in Which We are Engaged Is of Far More Importance, Ours is a Spiritual Warfare," *Church of God Evangel*, Feb. 24, 1917, p1.

Table of Contents

CHAPTER I
RELIGIOUS FERMENT IN THE LATE NINETEENTH AND EARLY TWENTIETH CENTURY AND THE ORIGINS OF PENTECOSTAL PACIFISM 1
   Two-Fold Nineteenth Century Roots
   to Pentecostalism 1
   Nineteenth Century Eschatology 2
   Holiness Roots of Pentecostal Pacifism ... 4
      Thomas Upham 4
      Amos Dresser 5
      Holiness Church Bodies 7
      Holiness Groups and Peace Churches . 10
      Contemporary Pacifistic Witness in the
      Holiness Movement 11
   Reformed Evangelical Roots 13
      Dwight L. Moody 13
   Other Sources of Pentecostal Pacifism .. 14

CHAPTER II
THE EXTENT OF PENTECOSTAL PACIFISM 21
   Pacifism in Various Pentecostal Groups .. 21
   Pacifism In Various Countries 32

CHAPTER III
MAJOR PERSONALITIES IN THE DEVELOPMENT OF PACIFISM IN PENTECOSTAL CIRCLES 37
   The Logic of the Early Leaders' Pacifism . 37
      John Alexander Dowie 38

Arthur Sydney Booth-Clibborn 41
Charles Fox Parham 51
Frank Bartleman 54
Stanley H. Frodsham 59
Donald Gee 60
Howard Carter 64

CHAPTER IV
MAJOR PERSONALITIES WHO MODERATED PACIFISM IN PENTECOSTAL CIRCLES 73
MODERATES 73
Eudorus N. Bell 73
Ernest S. Williams 77
Lycurgus Reuben Lynch 81
DETRACTORS 84
Alexander A. Boddy and
Cecil Polhill in Britain 84
Raymond T. Richey 88
OTHERS 90
The Tomlinsons 90
Ambrose Jessup Tomlinson 90

CHAPTER V
THE EXPERIENCE OF PENTECOSTALS IN THE WORLD WARS 97
WORLD WAR I 97
The Espionage and Sedition Acts 98
Clarence H. Waldron 98
William Reid 99
Charles H. Mason 100
Ambrose J. Tomlinson 100
Brother Schaffer 101

THE CONSCIENTIOUS OBJECTOR . . 101
   England 101
   United States 101
WORLD WAR II 103

CHAPTER VI
THE LOSS OF PENTECOSTAL PACIFISM 107
   The Change in Social Status 107
   World War II 109
   Active Duty in World War II 109
   Chaplaincy 110
   National Association of Evangelicals 111
   Assemblies of God Since World War II . . 112

CONCLUSION 123

BIBLIOGRAPHY 125

INDEX 135
   Name 135
   Religious Denominations/Movements . . . 137
   Subject 140

FOREWORD

There were good reasons, when in the 1930s the usage arose of grouping the Brethren, the Friends, and the Mennonites under the label "historic peace churches." Each of them bore the legacy of origins in the radicalizing of a renewal movement within protestant Europe. All three of them had been formed by the experience of colonial Pennsylvania. All three had retained an explicit official pacifist commitment despite ambivalences in the consistency of its practice by their members in times of war. The term seems to have arisen as a self-designation when a few of their leaders gathered in the mid-30s to face the threat of war to come. Each of them counted about 200,000 members in North America; despite repeated schisms each had a respectable denominational organization.

These commonalities - most of them nontheological, we note - made it easy for both "peace church" people themselves and others to proceed as if these three communions were integrally pacifist and as if Christian pacifism were limited to them. Both misapprehensions are harmful. Both belong to the "denominationalistic" error of correlating organizations and positions in a one-to-one way.

One resource for refuting the denominationalistic error is the actual experience of renewal, whereby under the pressure of the times, the Spirit, and the scriptures, new convictions arise where no body had represented them before. Sometimes these new beginnings create parachurch agencies, as with the Bible Societies, the YMCA, the Evangelical Alliance, Moody's mode of evangelization, or the "faith missions." Sometimes they create new non-historical denominations, as holiness revival largely did, and pentecostalism following it. However it settles out, the beginnings of such movements document the perennial openness toward change which the myth of denominational trueness-to-type tries to ward off.

That openness toward change is not a quality of a particular form of organization, although some forms may be more flexible than others. It is not a quality only of a particular form of deliberation or of worship, although some forms are less hidebound than others. The power for change is a work of God the Spirit, whose "blowing as it wills" (Jn 3:8) is not bound by the more or less appropriate forms we put at its disposal.

As the classical survey in Donald Durnbaugh's Believers' Church makes plain, there is a kind of "free church syndrome," a set of qualities which belong together to constitute the wholeness, the Gestalt of a new beginning. In different centuries the starting point differs. For Cheltchitsky and Michael Sattler, for George Fox and William Penn, for Alexander Campbell and the Booth-Clibborns, the point of conflict where the new movement broke off was different each time. Yet each time the same set of appropriate forms was worked out: adult voluntary membership, independence from state

Foreword

and hierarchy, worship centering in Bible reading and prayer, ministry disconnected from academic credentialing, ethical earnestness ... One component of this "free church syndrome" has regularly been pacifism, as Jay Beaman's pioneering work has solidly demonstrated in the holiness and pentecostal cases.

Ecumenically and historically, the holiness/pentecostal experience which Beaman recounts is more interesting than the classical "established" pacifism of the Historic Peace Churches. The props of a long history and a separate ethnic ethos make pacifism "normal" for Friends, Brethren, Hutterians, Mennonites. Arising without any such props, charismatic pacifism is a component of the first-generation transformation wrought by the synergy of enthusiasm and prima facie biblicism. The consciousness that their own pacifism is reinforced by or even logically dependent upon their sectarian history burdens Mennonites (perhaps more than Brethren or Friends) with doubt about whether it can be commended to fellow Christians or urged on the world. The pacifist who has come to that stance by first-generation convincement can be freed from such doubts. "You are freed from violence" is a part of the miracle of renewal. Pragmatism about social values to be defended politically is no more decisive than is determinism about whether hearts can be changed or sins forgiven.

Beaman is honest about the shadow side of the story he tells. Pentecostalism's changes have become a classical specimen of the "sect cycle," making within barely two generations some fundamental accommodations to establishment like those which took early Christianity centuries. The prima facie biblicism did not mature into a solid ethical hermeneutic. The prophetic discernment of the evils of social stratification yielded with astonishing ease to personal prosperity and institutional respectability. The millennial hope no longer functioned as existential grounds for nonconformity to the world, but can in fact flip over into an especially naive form of anticommunism (and sometimes Zionism). The ministry of women and "laity" subsided behind the credentialing of ministers (partially for military purposes). This parallels the loss of Pentecostalism's initial interracial character (not in Beaman's account). For some reason the sellout was slower in the British churches than in the States.

Beaman lays the foundation for further analysis of how the particular strengths and weaknesses of the pentecostal vision of renewal made the transition to uncritical patriotism easier. Does the subjectivism of Pentecostals make easier the idea that "conscience" is what determines the legitimacy of military service (E. S. Williams)? How has one's understanding of the Christian life been disconnected from the publishing of the Good News, when one says "It is none of our business to push our faith as to war on others... (E. N. Bell)"?

Once the initial simplicity is relinquished, the acceptance of national loyalty respects hardly any restraint. Majority Christians, when they accepted war, limited it (at least theoretically) by the "just war" criteria. Such limits do not show in the Pentecostals' case against pacifism, when war is juxtaposed with the death penalty, "executing the criminal Hun (Bell)." They do not show when the U.S. government is asked to extend the postwar occupation of Italy as a favor to Protestants there. They do not show in Pat Robertson's collecting quasi-covert subsidies for the contras, or in Jimmy Swaggart's affirming the legitimacy of the Pinochet regime. No special reproach should inhere in these observations; these modes of patriotic accommodation are in no way peculiar to Pentecostals. That is just the point; they are mainstream Christendom responses, unworthy of the nonconformist originality and spiritual independence with which the movement began.

Beaman, properly, does not carry through this analysis. He tells us just enough of the story to show us where it might begin. For this all church historians and all peace church leaders are in his debt.

John H. Yoder
Department of Theology University of Notre Dame

INTRODUCTION

Pacifism in Pentecostal circles was deeply rooted and broadly endorsed in the early history of the Pentecostal Movement and may be seen, however faintly, to this day. This is especially true in those Pentecostal groups which have resisted cultural conformity.

The pacifism of the early Pentecostals was closely related to their world view, especially eschatology, which informed much of their ethical behavior. Belief in the imminent return of Jesus colored their view of reality and fueled their motivation for missions. They were generally poor people. Their faith helped them cope with perilous times and gave them hope for a better life in the age to come.

A literal approach to the scriptures led to the distinctive Pentecostal practice of speaking in tongues and to an identification with the early church. The Pentecostals assumed the early church had taken the Sermon on the Mount literally with regard to nonresistance until the time of Constantine. They believed that the renewal of the church in modern times should include a return to those earlier pacific beliefs.

At the end of World War I, many Pentecostals moderated their eschatology and world view. In the course of time, upward social mobility altered their view of reality and interpretation of Scripture. Although many Pentecostal members today give little consideration to pacific beliefs, it is surprising how many Pentecostal denominations still hold official pacific statements.

No one has yet made a study of the origins of pacifism in the Pentecostal Movement. It is not a major concern with most Pentecostals today. At a time when the Evangelical wing of the church is beginning to show some signs of soul searching over the issues of war and peace, the Pentecostals would do well to study their own heritage. Whether they accept or reject their earlier world view, they need to interpret the motivation for their original beliefs and those which they now hold. As people of the word of God, have Pentecostals altered their pacific views as a result of new Biblical insights or cultural accommodation?

This study is an attempt to trace and interpret the rapid change of views on pacifism in the modern Pentecostal Movement.

CHAPTER I

RELIGIOUS FERMENT IN THE LATE NINETEENTH AND EARLY TWENTIETH CENTURY AND THE ORIGINS OF PENTECOSTAL PACIFISM

Two-Fold Nineteenth Century Roots to Pentecostalism

Any search for the roots of Pentecostal pacifism must begin with the immediate antecedents to Pentecostalism at the end of the nineteenth century; the Wesleyan Holiness Movement[1] and Reformed-evangelical revivalism.[2] Born at the beginning of the twentieth century, the Pentecostal Movement quickly divided over the issue of sanctification along lines provided by these two sources.[3] By the beginning of World War I in Europe, several Pentecostal groups had been organized into fledgling denominations. Chief among these early groups was the Assemblies of God, the Pentecostal Holiness Church, the Church of God (Cleveland), and the Church of God in Christ (black). By 1920, a 1916 controversy over trinitarian beliefs resulted in a unitarian Pentecostal sector of churches which would ultimately hold approximately one fourth of the Pentecostal adherents.[4] The main groups in the unitarian wing of Pentecostalism merged to become The United Pentecostal Church.

Nineteenth Century Eschatology

At least until the time of the Civil War, the Holiness Movement was predominantly postmillennial in eschatology. This belief was closely tied to the American experience. Timothy Smith notes that the revivalists rejected the idea of foreordination "as far as it concerned individuals." It "was now transferred to a grander object--the manifest destiny of a Christianized America." They envisioned converting and civilizing the globe while "purg[ing] society of all its evils," in preparation for "Christ's reign on earth." Smith notes the effect on the revivalists' social ethic: "The quest of personal Holiness became in some ways a kind of plain man's transcendentalism, which geared ancient creeds to the drive shaft of social reform." In attacking "slavery, poverty, and greed; they thus helped prepare the way both in theory and in practice for what later became known as the social gospel."[5]

While some Holiness people envisioned the work of the Spirit in sanctification bringing an end to organized sin such as "intemperance, slavery, and war,"[6] most Holiness people were so opposed to slavery that they approved of a war to end it. Even this fit their eschatology. War was seen as the judgment of Christ. "An awakened generation learned at Fredricksburg and Antietam a new understanding of 'the glory of the coming of the Lord.' Julia Ward Howe penned the unforgettable words and music, in her famous 'Battle Hymn.'"[7] However, it was only three decades later when Howe penned new words for the same tune:

> For the glory that we saw,
> In the battle flag unfurled,
> Let us read Christ's better law,
> Fellowship for all the world.[8]

She now rejected war as a Christian option.

In the same way, many Holiness people rejected war with time. Before the turn of the century the Holiness Movement also rejected postmillennialism, with its belief in the perfection of society. According to Donald Dayton, most historians trace this move from optimism to pessimism to "the impact of the Civil War and the collapse of the pre-war dream of a Christian America under the impact of immigration, industrialization and urbanization." Dayton also notes that during this time Holiness advocates started equating the experience of sanctification with that of the baptism in the Holy Ghost as mentioned in Acts 2. By "making Acts 2 (with its emphasis on the prophecy of Joel) the hermeneutical key to the whole of Scriptures," the Holiness Movement shifted emphasis to a "'prophetic' interpretation of the Bible," and thus "toward the new Prophecy Conference Movement that began in the 1870s."[9] The Prophecy Movement was strongly influenced by the pessimistic premillennialism of John Nelson Darby which had an other-worldly ethic. According to Reuben Torrey, "In the return of our Lord is the perfect solution, and the only solution, of the political and social and commercial problems that now vex us."[10] Instead of ideas of optimism and progress in society, there was the "idea of conflict between the Christian and the world." One was forced to make choices between "the Holy Spirit and the spirit of the age."¹¹ This set the stage for the kind of nonconformity required of a pacifist.

Holiness Roots of Pentecostal Pacifism

Melvin Dieter finds in the nineteenth-century Holiness revival a confluence of three streams: historic pietism, American revivalism, and Wesleyan perfectionism which were rooted in the pietism of Spener, Zinzendorf, and Bunyan. Yet this revival was a part of the "pragmatic American experiment." It was "a Wesleyan pietism oriented much more towards Christian activity than pietistic introspection." Dieter also notes that like the pietists, the Holiness Movement built their ethic on the New Testament in an "oppositive" or "over-against" manner of protesting the religious establishment.¹²

Thomas Upham

In 1838 Thomas Upham, a Congregationalist professor of mental and moral philosophy at Bowdin College, attended Phoebe Palmer's "Tuesday Meetings for the Promotion of Holiness." As a result, Upham experienced a "new state of Christian experience." Thus, Upham became the first vocal pacifist to join to the Holiness Movement. Two years previously, Upham published his *Manual of Peace*, which was an absolute statement of pacifism. Upham called for nonparticipation in war, avoidance of war taxes, and the abolition of capital punishment. Arguments were taken both from nature and scripture. He advocated civil disobedience if necessary, stating that "we wish to show ourselves good citizens in every possible way; but we ask to be exempted from compulsory disobedience to that great Lawgiver, whose commands should always take the precedence of those of every earthly legislator." In language that would express the feelings of Holiness people on a number of issues, Upham called for nonconformity. Upham urged Christians to refuse military service in war:

> While Christian soldiers mingle in its ranks and Christian chaplains pray for its success: on no subject is the cry louder and more urgent, 'Touch not the unclean thing. Come out and be separate.'[13]

Perhaps most significant in terms of this study is the part played by the millennium in Upham's work. He argued:

> The principles, which will be acknowledged as authoritative in the Millennium, are the very principles, which are prescribed, and are binding on us at the present moment. No change in principles is required; but merely a change in practice. If the practice of men should to-morrow be conformed to the principles, which the finger of God had written on the pages of the New Testament, then tomorrow would behold the Millennium.[14]

After Upham's experience at the "Tuesday Meetings," he began to write in a mystical vein. Not only did he bring the cause of Holiness to a much broader sector of the church, but he was responsible for introducing the Holiness Movement to such classic figures as Madame Guyon, the French Catholic mystic and friend of Fenelon.[15]

Amos Dresser

Although it is impossible to say whether Amos Dresser influenced the wider Holiness Movement on the issue of war, he did publish a book on the subject in 1849 titled *The Bible Against War*. This book shows the influence of Thomas Upham on Dresser. Dresser's book was a statement of pacifism, more absolute than Asa Mahan or Charles Finney, professors at Oberlin where Dresser was a student.[16] Dresser's view was also shaped by his postmillennial eschatology.[17] Significantly, while Dresser was antislavery, he did not sanction violence against the slave holder in any effort to emancipate the slave.[18] In the mid-1890s, Amos Dresser became a friend of John Alexander Dowie, who later founded Zion, Illinois. Amos Dresser, Jr., the son of Amos Dresser, became one of the elders in Dowie's Christian Catholic Church and the manager of Zion Publishing House.[19] There is no record that Amos Dresser directly influenced Dowie's views on pacifism, although Dowie published articles about Amos Dresser's abolitionist and anti-racist sentiments in Dowie's magazine, *Leaves of Healing*.[20] For Amos Dresser, the issues of racial justice and pacifism were connected as he made clear in his book, *The Bible Against War*.[21] John Alexander Dowie had a significant impact on early Pentecostals who followed Dowie's ministry before they became Pentecostals. Dowie became a pacifist within a few years of his friendship with Amos Dresser, but there is no direct evidence that Dowie's pacifism was learned from Amos Dresser. In fact, Dowie fired Amos Dresser, Jr., from his publishing enterprise and removed him from ministry in 1899 over a business disagreement.[22] John Alexander Dowie's pacifism and influence are treated in chapter three.

Holiness Church Bodies

Arthur Piepkorn's *Profiles in Belief* lists the many groups into which the Holiness Movement is divided. A surprising number of their statements show varying degrees of revulsion to war.[23]

As early as 1844, the Wesleyan Methodists were dealing with the issue of war in their *Discipline*. They noted that the gospel was in "every way opposed to the practice of war in all its forms; and those customs which tend to foster and perpetuate the war spirit, [are] inconsistent with the benevolent designs of the Christian Religion." The St. Lawrence Annual Conference of the Wesleyan Methodists commended the Quakers for showing "that love is a more powerful defense than physical force." They also considered a resolution "to alter the denominational *Discipline* so that refusal to engage in war and military training would become a condition of membership." The Wesleyan Methodist Church promoted peace until World War I, when they argued that "human war is undoubtedly the product of human sin, but it does not necessarily follow that all who engage in war are sinners."[24]

During World War I in England, the Church of the Nazarene "declared its abhorrence of war," but fell short of requiring members to refuse military service. However, shortly after the War, they developed a strong pacific strain that has lasted to some extent to the present.[25]

At the outbreak of World War I, the Free Methodists advocated peace, almost to the point of pacifism. The

East Michigan Conference in 1914 issued a statement of revulsion against the war couched in terms which may have shown a rejection of postmillennialism.

> War. Has Civilization perished from the earth? Have the ideals of Christianity, introduced two thousand years ago by the PRINCE OF PEACE, utterly failed? ... The appeal to the god of brute force is founded upon the basest elements in the nature of men. ... We are far short of the millennium, rather are we come to the fulfillment of prophecy in reference to the conditions preceding the coming of the Son of Man. We commend the efforts of the little nuclei of men who are endeavoring to bring about peaceful arbitration in the nations of the earth.[26]

Two years later the Genesee Conference rejected military preparedness, stating that:

> ... All modern wars have been brought about by avarice and greed. We believe the application of the golden rule to all our dealings with other nations and acting the part of the good Samaritan toward them in their destitution and suffering will give us the best protection and the most effectual preparedness we as a nation can have.[27]

At the same time, the Oil City Conference recognized the cessation of national war was "possibly the greatest reform... needed today." Deploring the cost in billions of dollars and millions of lives, the Oil City Conference asked what could be done. The answer was less than complete pacifism. They noted: "We can beseech the mercy of the Lord on this blood-stained world. We can vote for men who stand for truth and righteousness. We can refuse to manufacture war supplies."[28] The events of 1917 brought a response from no less than seven Free Methodist conferences on the subject of war and related themes. The Genesee Conference called military spending and training "satanic."[29] The 1917 *Annual Minutes* reveal something of the social status of the Holiness

Movement of that day by its stinging rebuke of capitalism:

> The world has long been cursed by an economic system that has stood as a bulwark against human progress, and for the sake of sordid gain has fostered well nigh every vice known to man. For ages, millions of laborers upon whom it depends for success in exploitation have seldom been free from the pinch of hunger: sties they have for homes: barred from the so-called best society, prevented from securing either a healthy body or a well-trained mind, blighted in birth and damned through life, the procession of wrong human progeny continues because of an economic system that can not be justified by either political science, moral philosophy or the Christian religion. Equality is the only rightful relation between human beings and that can never obtain so long as the masses are slaves of the classes. The capitalistic system is an economic outrage, a political fraud, and a giant leech on society. We commend the efforts of our President to cope with this great evil and pledge ourselves to the overthrow of this barrier to human progress and to the ushering in of a just regime when the laborer who is worthy of his hire shall receive the just reward of his toil.[30]

While there were examples of this kind of thinking among secular critics, this prophetic analysis could have just as easily come from the pen of Walter Rauschenbusch. This critique of capitalism was tinged with the vestiges of postmillennial thought, and bears witness to the fact that the lines between pietism and the social gospel were not clearly drawn at this time.

While the Free Methodists were not consistently pacific as a Movement, there were those within the Movement who were. "One center of this seems to have been E. E. Shelhamer and his Reparier Publishing Company in Atlanta, Georgia. During World War I, the *Repairer* and the *Herald of Light* both published an article by W. S. Craig advocating nonresistance, warning: "O Reader, don't let the devil fool you on this false notion of patriotism. . . . Will we, followers of the Prince of Peace, dedicate our bodies to the god of war?"[31]

Holiness Groups and Peace Churches

One reason Holiness people began to take seriously the peace witness may have been the influence of Quakers with whom the Holiness Movement was in association. There was a significant interplay between various sectors of the Holiness Movement, so that historic peace churches were affected by the Holiness Movement and the Holiness Movement was affected by the peace churches.[32] Charles Jones finds the 1946 statement of the Pilgrim Holiness Church on war, comparable with that of the Ohio Yearly Meeting of Friends in supporting "individual conscience."[33] However, the Emmanuel Association, which split from the Pilgrim Holiness Church, completely rejected military service. They state that members "cannot participate in war, war activities, or compulsory military training."[34]

The Church of God (Anderson, Indiana) was originally a peace church.[35] This group owes its origin to Daniel Warner, who was born in Ohio in 1842.[36] Warner seems to have been influenced by the geographical proximity and resultant contacts with Mennonites, Dunkards, and Anabaptists.[37] Warner worked for ten years in the Church of God (Winebrennerian), which "associated for a short time with the Northern Indiana Eldership of the Church of God." During this time Warner participated in talks for the purpose of merging this particular "Church of God" with the United Mennonite Church. During the process, Warner "spent several days of serious discussion with a Mennonite group about the nature of the church."[38]

This is an example of the close relationship of certain Mennonite groups and the Holiness Movement. The United Mennonites were merged with three other Holiness-related Mennonite churches to form the United Missionary Church in 1883. The United Missionary Church merged in 1966 with the Missionary Church Association, which was formed in 1898.

> One of the most influential among the founders of the association was the General Conference Mennonite minister, A. E. Funk, who was a close associate of A. B. Simpson, founder of the Christian Missionary Alliance.[39]

The Missionary Church Association stated in 1898 that "we believe it is contrary to the teachings of Christ and the New Testament for Christians to take up arms in war, revenge and self-defense."[40] Although Funk and Simpson were quite close, the available evidence does not suggest that the Christian and Missionary Alliance ever took a stand against members going to war.[41]

Contemporary Pacifistic Witness in the Holiness Movement

One Anabaptist group, the Brethren in Christ, became a part of the Holiness Movement. In 1887 the Brethren in Christ adopted a statement on sanctification which was typically Wesleyan,[42] yet they have remained true to their pacifism. According to Dayton, the Brethren in Christ are "now perhaps the only major Holiness body with a firm statement of nonresistance as a guiding principle."[43]

Although there is little evidence of their practical application, several smaller Holiness groups still carry strong pacific statements today. The Church of God (Guthrie, Oklahoma) believes that "separation from the world precludes all participation in war, including noncombatant service in the armed forces and military training."[44] The Churches of God (Independent Holiness People) reject "the use of carnal weapons in putting down violence." They are conscientious objectors "to any means whatsoever in killing any human being in war."[45] The Fire Baptized Holiness Church (Wesleyan) is "strictly opposed to war," and rejects the idea that its members "should be compelled to engage in combat services."[46] Christ's Sanctified Holy Church (West Columbia, South Carolina) disallows members participating in war and taking "up arms or train[ing] with [the] same."[47] A group of recent origin, the Gospel Mission Corps, affirms "obedience to appropriate authority," while refusing to take oaths or take up arms for the "purpose of destroying human life."[48]

Two groups allowing members to participate in noncombatant service are the Sanctified Church of Christ and the Bible Holiness Movement.[49]

The Holiness Christian Church of the United States of America Incorporated calls for settling international differences by arbitration.[50]

While it is impossible to substantiate the degree to which members of the various Holiness denominations have in the past or presently practice nonresistance to war, their literature gives ample testimony to a strong aversion to war and participation in war by Holiness people. The Holiness Movement provided the strongest and most direct roots for Pentecostal pacifism.[51]

Reformed Evangelical Roots To Pentecostal Pacifism

Reformed Evangelical roots for Pentecostal pacifism are less obvious. Plymouth Brethren and those groups which divided from the Plymouth Brethren contained active strains of pacific belief. This was due primarily to their biblical literalism.[52] Many Open Brethren in England became conscientious objectors in both World Wars.[53] The statement on war by Churches of God in the Fellowship of the Son of God, the Lord Jesus Christ notes that "the Lord's disciple cannot . . . become a soldier of an earthly king or government to engage in war . . . he may not serve in . . . army . . . either combatant or non-combatant".[54]

There is no evidence that Pentecostals borrowed their statement on war from Plymouth Brethren; but early Pentecostals would have been comfortable with similarities to Plymouth Brethren.[55]

Dwight L. Moody

Dwight L. Moody was a conscientious objector during the Civil War.[56] He said, "There has never been a time in my life when I felt that I could take a gun and shoot down a fellow being. In this respect I am a Quaker."[57] There were also in Moody's following some who espoused pacifism. Significantly, the only testimony to this is a quotation from the pacifist pamphlet read into a sedition trial during World War I. The man on trial was Clarence Waldren, a Pentecostal who was formerly a Baptist. The pamphlet was advertised in Moody's *Christian Worker Magazine*.[58] It was titled, *The Word of the Cross: Christ*

Again Before the Tribunal.[59] The text of the pamphlet, taken from the trial, reads:

> Surely, if Christians were forbidden to fight to preserve the Person of their Lord and Master, they may not fight to preserve themselves, or any city they should happen to dwell in. Christ has no kingdom here. His servants must not fight. The Christian may not go to "the front" to repel the foe for there he is required to kill men.
>
> They (referring to the Twelve Apostles) knew the force of the Lord's example, and whether to save themselves or to save others--- never, never use the sword.
>
> Better a thousand times to die than for a Christian to kill his fellow.
>
> I do not say that it is wrong for a nation to go to war to preserve its interests, but it is wrong to the Christian, absolutely, unutterably wrong.
>
> Under no circumstances can I undertake any service that has for its purpose the prosecution of war.[60]

Other Sources of Pentecostal Pacifism

Another source of pacific thinking in the nineteenth century was the Disciples of Christ and their leader Alexander Campbell.[61] Campbell maintained absolute pacifism throughout the Civil War.[62] In an article written in 1823 he discussed his views on war:

> And stranger still, see that Christian general, with his ten thousand soldiers, and his chaplain at his elbow, preaching, as he says, the gospel of good will among men; and hear him exhort his general and his Christian warriors to go forth with the Bible in one hand and the sword in the other to fight the battles of God and their country; praying that the Lord would cause them to fight valiantly, and render their efforts successful in making as many widows and orphans as will afford sufficient opportunity for others to manifest the purity of their religion by taking care of them!!![63]

The Disciples were a restorationist movement calling for a return to the apostolic church in the tradition of the Anabaptists. While there is no evidence of historical connections to the Pentecostal Movement, there is ideological similarity.[64]

In reviewing the widespread, yet not consistent, pacifism of the nineteenth and early twentieth century antecedents to Pentecostalism, it would seem surprising if pacifism had not been found among the Pentecostals. The Pentecostals owed a large debt to the Holiness and Reformed Evangelical sectors of the church in the nineteenth century for other beliefs as well as pacifism. If pacifism was a mark of sectarian separation, then the Pentecostals who separated to form a more vital church could be expected to outdo their predecessors.

Footnotes

1. Donald W. Dayton, "Theological Roots of Pentecostalism," *Pneuma: The Journal of the Society for Pentecostal Studies*, 2 (Spring 1980): 3-21; Melvin E. Dieter, "Wesleyan-Holiness Aspects of Pentecostal Origins: As Mediated Through the Nineteenth-Century Holiness Revival," in *Aspects of Pentecostal-Charismatic Origins*, ed. Vinson Synan (Plainfield, N.J.: Logos International, 1974), pp. 55-80; Vinson Synan, *The Holiness Pentecostal Movement in the United States* (Grand Rapids: William B. Eerdmans Publishing Co., 1971).

2. William W. Menzies, "The Non-Wesleyan Origins of the Pentecostal Movement," in *Aspects of Pentecostal-Charismatic Origins*, ed. Vinson Synan, pp. 81-98; Edith Waldvogel, "The 'Overcoming Life': A Study in the Reformed Evangelical Origins of Pentecostalism: (Ph.D. Thesis, Harvard University, 1977).

3. David W. Faupel, *The American Pentecostal Movement: A Bibliographic Essay*. (Wilmore, Ky.: Asbury Theological Seminary, 1972), p. 44-45.

4. Arthur Carl Piepkorn, *Profiles in Belief*, Vol 3 (N.Y.: Harper and Row, 1979), pp. 195-219.

5. Timothy L. Smith, *Revivalism and Social Reform: In Mid-Nineteenth-Century America* (New York: Abingdon Press, 1957), pp. 7f. Of course postmillennialism was not confined to Wesleyan holiness circles.

6. *Ibid.*, p. 152, citing *Watchman and Reflector*, March 23, 1854; a Baptist publication.

7. *Ibid.*, p. 232, notes that there was an inner dilemma for the Evangelical antislavery movement in "whether Christians might do violence for loving ends;" p. 188.

8. Merle E. Curti, *Peace or War: The American Struggle 1636-1936* (New York: Garland Publishing, Inc., 1972), p. 116.

9. Dayton, "Theological Roots," p. 18; Ernest R. Sandeen, *The Roots of Fundamentalism* (Chicago: University of Chicago Press, 1970). Thus the two sources of Pentecostalism were not distinct.

10. Waldvogel, p. 16, citing Reuben A. Torrey, *The Return of the Lord Jesus* (Los Angeles, 1913), p. 7.

11. *Ibid.*, p. 30.

12. Melvin Easterday Dieter, *The Holiness Revival of the Nineteenth-Century*, Studies in Evangelicalism, vol. 1 (Metuchen, N. J.: Scarecrow Press, 1980), p. 4; significantly, Moravians have been pacifists since 1450; see Werner Stark, *Sociology of Religion*, vol. 2 (New York: Fordham University Press, 1967), p. 210.

13. Thomas C. Upham, *Manual of Peace* (New York: Leavitt, Lord & Co., 1836; reprint ed., The Peace Movement in America Collection, n.p.: Jerome S. Ozer, Pub., 1972), pp. 41-43, 81, 85, 98, 162-170, punctuation changed for clarity on p. 171.

14. *Ibid.*, p. 144.

15. Dieter, p. 53-55. The degree to which Upham influenced the Holiness Movement is not certain because many feared his strong mystical bent. However, his book *The Life and Experience of Madame Guyon*, was advertised in the *Pentecostal Evangel*, August 2, 1924, p. 16. Nothing suggests the Pentecostals were reading his *Manual of Peace*.

16. Amos Dresser, *The Bible Against War* (Oberlin: Printed for author, 1849; Louisville : Lost Cause Press, microcard, 1962), pp. v-x.

17. *Ibid.*, pp. xii, 252.

18. *Ibid.*, pp. 254, 265-276.

19. *Leaves of Healing*, Vol. 3, Jan. 8, 1897, p. 183.
20. *Leaves of Healing*, Vol. 3, Apr. 24, 1897, pp. 414-5; Leaves of Healing, Vol. 3, Ag. 14, 1897, pp. 657-662.
21. Amos Dresser, *The Bible Against War*.
22. *Leaves of Healing*, Vol. 5, Apr. 8, 1899, p. 450; Sept. 16, 1899, p. 915.
23. Arthur Carl Piepkorn, *Profiles in Belief*, vol. 3 (New York: Harper & Row, 1979), pp. 3-63.
24. Donald Dayton and Lucille S[ider] Dayton, "An Historical Survey of Attitudes Toward War and Peace Within the American Holiness Movement," (unpublished paper read to the Seminar on Christian Holiness and the Issues of War and Peace, Winona Lake, Indiana, June 7-9, 1973), pp. 7-89, 17; citing the following: Discipline of the Wesleyan Methodist Connection, 1844, p. 98; St. Lawrence Annual Conference "Minutes," (handwritten), 1847, available in the library of Houghton College, Houghton, New York; Dr. Wilbur Crofts, The Wesleyan Methodist, June 30, 1915, p. 1; The Wesleyan Methodist, October 13, 1915, pp. 8-9; this paper was later published in *Perfect Love and War; A Dialogue on Christian Holiness and the Issues of War and Peace* (Nappanee Indiana: Evangel Press, 1974) 132-152. This paper by the Daytons is the only resource of its kind covering the holiness movement.
25. Jack Ford, *In the Steps of John Wesley: The Church of the Nazarene in Britain* (Kansas City, Mo.: Nazarene Publishing House, 1968), pp. 152-153, 209-210.
26. *Annual Minutes: Combined Number 1914* (Chicago: Free Methodist Publishing House, 1914), p. 61.
27. *Annual Minutes*, 1916, p. 189.
28. *Ibid.*, p. 243.
29. *Annual Minutes*, 1917, p. 220; this year's entries also give a great deal of contrary evidence. With the U.S. entry to the war, patriotism became fashionable. The New York Conference took the lead giving America a place of cosmic significance in history, and pledging loyalty to the government. Preachers were admonished not to discuss the war issue, p. 367. The Susquehana Conference implied that this was a "just war," p. 349. The Oil City Conference displayed patriotism, yet warned against "trusting alone in the arm of the flesh," n.p. Three other conferences, however, gave statements deploring the war, pp. 113, 186, 305.
30. *Ibid.*, p. 304
31. Dayton, "War and Peace," pp. 18-20; citing E. O. Jolley, *Under Higher Orders* (Atlanta: Repairer Publishing Co., n.d.), pp. 26-33,

72-76. Craig was dependent on the work of A. S. Booth-Clibborn who is treated in Chapter III in this book.

32. Dieter, *Holiness Revival*, p. 39; Robert Pearsall Smith and Hannah Whitall Smith were Quakers, p. 187; Robert Wilson, one of the founders of the Keswick Convention, was a Quaker, p. 191; Charles Jones gives numerous examples of the effect of the holiness movement on the Quakers, *Perfectionist Persuasion: The Holiness Movement and American Methodism*, 1867-1936, ATLA Monograph Series, no. 5 (Metuchen, N. J.: Scarecrow Press, 1974), pp. 60f, 113.

33. Charles Edwin Jones, *Perfectionist Persuasion*, p. 178.

34. *Ibid.*, p. 135; Piepkorn, *Profiles in Belief*, p. 51, citing *Principles of Holy Living* (n.p., n.d.), p. 11-16; this statement which originates later than the Pentecostal statements is still witness to pacifism that at times was prevalent in the holiness movement. Likely the Emmanuel Association formed in reaction to a perceived loss in holiness standards in the Pilgrim Holiness Church. The statement on war is part of a whole list prohibiting dances, theaters, horse races, church picnics and socials, radio and television.

35. Dayton, "War and Peace," p. 22.

36. Dieter, *Holiness Revival*, p. 245-257.

37. *Ibid.*, p. 254; Warner mentions preaching to "Dunkards and other peace groups."

38. *Ibid.*, p. 255; This Church of God is not to be confused with that of Anderson, Indiana, which was started by Warner in 1881; see Piepkorn, vol. 3, p. 21. Warner associated closely with Mennonites and his book, *Bible Proofs*, was published by the Evangelical Mennonite Publishing House at Goshen, Indiana; see Dieter, p. 285.

39. Piepkorn, vol. 4, pp. 21-23; although the name was the Mennonite Brethren in Christ until 1947.

40. A. Stauffer Curry, *Statements of Religious Bodies on the Conscientious Objector* (Washington, D.C.: National Service Board for Religious Objectors, 1953), pp. 43-44.

41. Simpson was also influenced by Presbyterian roots. A large number of ministers came out of the Christian and Missionary Alliance into the Assemblies of God when the latter was formed. There is every possibility that they were influenced by their Anabaptist contacts in the holiness movement; see Menzies, *Anointed to Serve*, p. 72; Carl Brumback, *Suddenly From Heaven: A History of the Assemblies of God* (Springfield, Mo.: Gospel Publishing House, 1961), p. 93.

42. Carlton O. Wittlinger, *Quest for Piety and Obedience: The Story of the Brethren in Christ* (Nappanee, Ind.: Evangel Press, 1978), p. 231.

Religious Ferment In The Nineteenth Century 19

43. Dayton, "War and Peace," p. 21.

44. Piepkorn, *Profiles in Belief*, vol. 3, p. 22; citing Lawrence D. Pruitt, *The Christian Versus War* (pamphlet, n.p., n.d.); Stauffer, *Statements of Religious Bodies on the Conscientious Objector*, p. 18, extensive 1948 statement. This church came out of the (then pacifist) Church of God (Anderson, Indiana) in 1910.

45. Piepkorn, vol. 3, p. 27; citing "The Convention of 1967," *The Church Advocate and Good Way*, vol. 51, no. 42 (October 26, 1967), p. 2. This group formed in 1920.

46. *Ibid.*, pp. 31-32; citing *Articles of Faith and By-Laws, The Fire Baptized Holiness Church* (n.p., 1963) (63 page pamphlet), pp. 39-43. This church formed out of Methodists and Friends in Southern Kansas in the 1890s.

47. *Ibid.*, pp. 32-33, 67; citing "Statements of Christ's Sanctified Holy Church Concerning War" (1 page undated multilithed document). This group originated in 1892. See also Stauffer, pp. 15-16, for a lengthy pacifist statement from 1893.

48. *Ibid.*, pp. 57-58; citing Article VIII ("Doctrine"), Constitution, Manual of the Gospel Mission Corps, Incorporated (Cranbury, N. J.: Gospel Mission Corps, n.d.), pp. 9-13. This group formed in the 1960s from ministers of "Pillar of Fire, Pilgrim Holiness (now Wesleyan) and Mennonite Brethren in Christ churches."

49. *Ibid.*, pp. 49, 55; citing *Discipline of Sanctified Church of Christ* (2nd printing: Columbus, Ga.: Sanctified Church of Christ, 1957), pp. 10-11; this group dates to 1937; also citing letter from Wesley H. Wakefield, president; This group traces to Vancouver, B.C., in 1947.

50. *Ibid.*, p. 36; citing "Articles of Faith and General Rules," *The Doctrines and Discipline of the Holiness Christian Church of the United States of America, Incorporated* (n.p., 1948), (74 page brochure), pp. 9-19; 57-58.

51. Dayton, "War and Peace," p. 17.

52. Although the Plymouth Brethren have since rejected the dispensational eschatology of their early preacher, John Nelson Darby, their pacific views may have been related (as were those of the Pentecostals) to their pessimistic premillennialism. However, there is little evidence to suggest this.

Anthony Norris Groves, early leader and contemporary of Darby, was a pacifist; see F. Roy Coad, *A History of the Brethren Movement: Its Origins, Its Worldwide Development and Its Significance for the Present Day* (Exeter: Paternoster Press, 1968) p. 22; p. 61 tells of Percy Francis Hall, of Plymouth, who "put forward his views in a booklet entitled Discipleship, in which he adopted extreme pacifist grounds."

53. George Henry Lang, *An Ordered Life* (London: Paternoster Press, 1959), pp. 173-175.

54. Piepkorn, vol. 4, pp. 32-34; citing Gordon Willis and Bryan R. Wilson, "The Churches of God: Pattern and Practice," in Bryan R. Wilson, ed., *Patterns of Sectarianism: Organization and Ideology in Social and Religious Movements* (London: Heinemann's Educational Books, 1967), p. 281; note also the early name used unofficially by this group, "the Assemblies of God in the British Isles," and the similarity to the Pentecostal denominational name.

55. Some similarities between the two groups: (1) dispensational eschatology, (2) congregational names (assemblies), and (3) biblical literalism.

56. Dayton, "War and Peace," pp. 1-2; Dayton notes that Moody's pacifism was suppressed in the later edition of *The Life of D. L. Moody*.

57. *What About Church History?*, ed. Willard E. Roth, peacemaker pamphlet no. 4 (Scottsdale, Penn.: Herald Press, 1964), p. 14.

58. Harold L. Rotzel, "Vermont's Sedition Trial," *New York Evening Post*, 4 February 1918, p. 9: also notes that it was advertised in a "Northfield publication of Moody interests, *The Record of Christian Work*." The other aspects of this trial will be treated in Chapter V, of this book.

59. *Ibid.*

60. Ray H. Abrams, *Preachers Present Arms*, rev. and enl. (Scottdale, Penn.: Herald Press, 1969), p. 215; Zechariah Chafee, *Freedom of Speech* (New York: Harcourt, Brace and Company, n.d.), pp. 61-62. The Pentecostal Movement had a great deal of respect for Moody and his associates, especially Torrey; see Waldvogel, "The 'Overcoming Life.'"

61. *The New International Dictionary of the Christian Church*, s.v. "Alexander Campbell." Robert G. Clouse; they were called "Campbellites."

62. Alfred T. DeGroot, *Disciple Thought: A History* (Fort Worth: Author, 1965) p. 1689; Campbell's pacifism in the Civil War is not surprising, since he was not an abolitionist.

63. *Ibid.*, p. 167.

64. Winfred Ernest Garrison and Alfred T. DeGroot, *The Disciples of Christ: A History*, rev. ed. (St. Louis: Bethany Press, 1964), p. 335.

CHAPTER II

THE EXTENT OF PENTECOSTAL PACIFISM

While the early Pentecostal Movement did not require pacifism from members, most early Pentecostal groups give evidence of official pacifist belief. There were open differences of opinion, but overwhelming pacifist belief characterized the movement. The literary witness to such beliefs remains as tacit evidence of the support for pacifism by the key leaders in each group represented.[1] Some groups which have changed their statements on pacifism retain vestiges of earlier beliefs.

Most pacifist statements originated at the time of World War I because of a need for Pentecostal groups to know how to respond to the war. As a result, many groups in existence at that time formulated their beliefs in relation to World War I. Some Pentecostal groups listed have since changed their beliefs. In a number of cases, this change is dealt with in the final chapter.

Evidences of Pacifism in Various Pentecostal Groups

An analysis of Pentecostal groups is complex because of the large number of Pentecostal bodies. This chapter will follow what is now a commonplace categorization of Pentecostal denominations, found in David W. Faupel's essay, *The American Pentecostal Movement: a Bibliographic Essay*. Faupel gives a three-fold categorization of Pentecostalism:

1. Those denominations which hold a Keswick view of sanctification.
2. Those denominations which hold a Holiness view of "entire sanctification."
3. Those denominations which hold a "Jesus Only" view of the God-head.[2]

A Keswick understanding of sanctification, following the Keswick Convention in England and the Dwight L. Moody revival meetings in the United States at the end of the nineteenth century, was baptistic in its view of sanctification. This model collapsed the crisis of sanctification with the conversion experience. In this view, the major work of sanctification was progressive throughout the Christian life. Pentecostals who followed this perspective believed that conversion is followed by the baptism in the Holy Spirit. The Assemblies of God is the prototypical denomination of this grouping.

A Holiness view of sanctification, "entire sanctification," derives from the Holiness Movement at the end of the nineteenth century. Those adopting this view believed that the work of sanctification was a crisis experience and a second work of grace following conversion. Pentecostals of this variety simply added the third step of the baptism in the Holy Spirit accompanied by glossolalia or speaking in tongues. The Pentecostal Holiness Church and the Church of God (Cleveland, Tennesee) are prototypical of this grouping, as is the Church of God in Christ, the largest black Pentecostal denomination.

The Extent of Pentecostal Pacifism

Both of the previous divisions reflected the revivalistic options at the turn of the century. The Holiness option was initially the most popular among Pentecostals, and the choice of the Keswick option was a major division from what was then the norm of a three-stage view of the conversion process.

Another division of the Movement led to a third grouping of Pentecostals. This division was over christology. In 1916 a number of the Keswick variety of Pentecostals took a unitarian view of God centering on a "Jesus Only" interpretation of the baptismal formula. These came to be identified as the Oneness Pentecostal Denominations or the Jesus Only Pentecostals. The United Pentecostal Church has become prototypical of this grouping.

The logic of these two divisions over christology and sanctification and the three resulting groupings can be represented in Table 2.1.

Table 2.1
SANCTIFICATION AND TIME

Christology	CRISIS Three Stage Process a. Conversion b. Sanctification c. Baptism in the Spirit	PROGRESSIVE Two Stage Process a. Conversion b. Baptism in the Spirit
TRINITARIAN	Wesleyan or Holiness Pentecostal Holiness Church Church of God (Cleveland) Church of God in Christ (black)	Keswick or Baptistic Assemblies of God
UNITARIAN		Oneness Pentecostal Denominations (baptism in the name of Jesus) United Pentecostal Church

On April 28th, 1917, with the entry of the United States into World War I, the Executive and General Presbytery of the Assemblies of God passed a resolution which was to remain their "official" position on war until 1967. This detailed statement was to become a model after which others fashioned their statements. The text in full read:

> Resolution Concerning the Attitude of the General Council of the Assemblies of God Toward any Military Service which Involves the Actual Participation in the Destruction of Human Life.
>
> While recognizing Human Government as of Divine ordination and affirming our unswerving loyalty to the Government of the United States, nevertheless we are constrained to define our position with reference to the taking of human life.
>
> WHEREAS, in the Constitutional Resolution adopted at the Hot Springs General Council, April 1-10, 1914, we plainly declare the Holy Inspired Scriptures to be the all-sufficient rule of faith and practice, and
>
> WHEREAS the Scriptures deal plainly with the obligations and relations of humanity, setting forth the principles of "Peace on earth, good will toward men." (Luke 2:14); and
>
> WHEREAS we, as followers of the Lord Jesus Christ, the Prince of Peace, believe in implicit obedience to the Divine commands and precepts which instruct us to "Follow peace with all men," (Heb. 12:14); "Thou shalt not kill," (Exod. 20:13); "Resist not evil," (Matt. 5:39); "Love your enemies," (Matt.5:44): etc. and
>
> WHEREAS these and other Scriptures have always been accepted and interpreted by our churches as prohibiting Christians from shedding blood or taking human life;
>
> THEREFORE we, as a body of Christians, while purposing to fulfill all the obligations of loyal citizenship, are nevertheless constrained to declare we cannot conscientiously participate in war and armed resistance which involves the actual destruction of human life, since this is contrary to our view of the clear teachings of the inspired Word of God, which is the sole basis of our faith.[3]

While the statement was absolute in tone, there was no attempt to enforce it upon every member of the congregation even where there was disagreement.[4] The Assemblies of God was the prototype of the baptistic or Keswick doctrinal group regarding their belief on sanctification. They believed in a two-staged conversion process. Of the Keswick groups existent today, six give clear evidence of pacifist history.[5] These six are represented in Table 2.2.

Table 2.2

KESWICK PENTECOSTAL DENOMINATIONS WITH HISTORY OF PACIFISM DENOMINATION

1. Assemblies of God*
2. Calvary Pentecostal Church
3. Church of God of the Union Assembly
4. Filipino Assemblies of the First-Born
5. General Assembly and Church of the First Born
6. Olzabal Latin-American Council of Churches

*Pacifist until 1967

Four other Keswick denominations leave the matter of military service up to the individual's conscience. The statement in each case is structured in such a way that it appears to be a replacement for an earlier pacifist statement. The change is similar to the change made by the Assemblies of God in 1967, which now allows the individual to choose. The four denominations allowing individual choice are; the Christ Faith Mission, the Full Gospel Church Association, the General Council, the Christian Church of North America, and the Latin-American Council of the Pentecostal Church of God. The latter denomination does not allow political participation.[6]

In 1917, the Church of God (Cleveland, Tennessee) adopted a position "against members going to war."[7] The Pentecostal Holiness Church was initially a pacifist denomination.[8] Two groups which came out of the Pentecostal Holiness Church, the Congregational Holiness Church and the Fire Baptized Holiness Church, adopted a position against going to war.[9] The Congregational Holiness Church maintained loyalty to the government but claimed that "God's children should not take up arms against their fellowman."[10]

Table 2.3

HOLINESS PENTECOSTAL DENOMINATIONS WITH PACIFIST HISTORY

1. Church of God (Cleveland, Tennesee)*
2. Church of God (1957 Reformation)
3. Church of God (Mountain Assembly)
4. Church of God in Christ (Black)
5. Church of God of the Apostolic Faith
6. Church of God, Huntsville, Alabama
7. Churches of God of the Original Mountain Assembly
8. Congregational Holiness Church
9. Emmanuel Holiness Church
10. International Church of Christ
11. Original Church of God
12. Pentecostal Fire Baptized Holiness Church
13. Pentecostal Holiness Church**

*Pacifist until 1945
**Pacifist until 1941

The Church of God in Christ (Black) was founded by C. H. Mason (1863- 1961), the son of former slaves.[11] They "believe the shedding of human blood or taking of human life to be contrary to the teaching of our Lord and Savior, and as a body, [they] are adverse to war in all its various forms." This group presents themselves for service which "will not conflict with our conscientious scruples in this respect, with love to all, with malice toward none, and with due respect to all who differ from us in our interpretation of the Scriptures."[12] Table 2.3 shows the Holiness Pentecostal denominations with pacifist history.[13]

A smaller black Pentecostal group was significant in the way it distinguished itself from white churches by its pacifism. Walter J. Hollenweger quotes the following dialogue:

> Q. Was there another Church in the earth before Triumph?
> A. Yes. Church Militant.
> Q. Is there any difference between the Triumph Church and Church Militant?
> A. Yes. Church Militant is a Church of warfare, and Triumph is a Church of Peace.
> Q. What happened to Church Militant when Triumph was revealed?
> A. God turned it upside down and emptied His Spirit into Triumph.
> Q. Is Triumph just a Church only?
> A. No. It has a kingdom with it.[14]

The Church of God (Apostolic, 1901) is a black church which does not consider itself Pentecostal. However, its statement on speaking in tongues, as well as its view on the Trinity, are the same as oneness Pentecostal denominations. The Church of God (Apostolic, 1901) calls for members to live in "obedience to the laws of the land, but not in war and going to war."[15]

The Church of the Lord Jesus Christ of the Apostolic Faith, founded in 1919, holds an absolute view. Not only is it opposed to combatant and noncombatant service, but also wearing military uniforms and pledging allegiance to the flag. This group is multi-racial, yet predominantly black. It is part of the oneness sector of Pentecostalism.[16]

Table 2.4

ONENESS PENTECOSTAL DENOMINATIONS WITH A HISTORY OF PACIFISM

1. Apostolic Gospel Church of Jesus Christ (Bible Apostolic Church)
2. Assemblies of the Lord Jesus Christ
3. Associated Brotherhood of Christians
4. Church of God (Apostolic) (Black Holiness)
5. Church of Jesus Christ
6. Church of Jesus Christ Ministerial Alliance
7. Church of Jesus Christ of Georgia
8. Church of our Lord Jesus Christ of the Apostolic Faith
9. Pentecostal Assemblies of the World
10. United Pentecostal Church International

Other oneness Pentecostal groups take a similar stand against participation in war. The United Pentecostal Church has a statement modeled after the Assemblies of God. Oneness groups derive from a defection from the Assemblies of God. The statement by the United Pentecostal Church recognizes the validity of human government, but on the basis of a number of scriptures takes a position against "participating in combatant service in war."[17] The Pentecostal Assemblies of the World, Incorporated, believes they are not "to take up any weapon of destruction to slay another, whether in our own defense or the defense of others." Yet, they imply that it would be possible to serve in noncombatant capacity.[18] While the Church of the Little Children holds to conscientious objection, and does not allow noncombatant service, the local churches do not enforce this ruling.[19] Most oneness Pentecostal groups have a stand against going to war, yet allow noncombatant service.[20] The Apostolic Gospel Church of Jesus Christ is more absolute, stating, "We cannot take up arms against any man or support those who do so: therefore our members do not serve in the armed forces."[21] Table 2.4 lists the Oneness Pentecostal Denominations with a history of pacifism.[22]

A number of unclassified Pentecostal groups also had similar statements on war. The Mt. Sinai Holy Church of America, Incorporated, "takes a strong stand against war."[23] Many other smaller groups made similar statements against going to war, with a number of them allowing noncombatant service.[24]

Not all Pentecostal churches adopted a position against participation in war. The many groups which did have a statement against going to war, usually allowed members to go to war in noncombatant capacities. The reason for this will be more clear upon examination of the laws concerning conscientious objection during World War I.

The author has analyzed the belief statements of 117 Pentecostal denominations which are predominantly identified with United States and United States Territorial geography. Much of the evidence is garnered from Piepkorn's book, *Profiles in Belief*. Many of the denominations give no information about their views on war. For others, the contemporary evidence does not tell of historical stances relative to war. The evidence from Piepkorn was supplemented when possible from historical and denominational sources. The following findings are limited by the availability of evidence.

Thirty-eight of the 117 Pentecostal denominations, or 32.5%, give some evidence of pacifism at some point in their history. As recently as 1979, with the publication of of Piepkorn's book, *Profiles in Belief*, 34 of 117 denominations, or 29.1% held to some form of pacifism. Three groups which have changed their belief on pacifism are three of the largest and most significant Pentecostal denominations; The Assemblies of God, The Pentecostal Holiness Church, and the Church of God (Cleveland, Tennesee).

An analysis of the dates in which denominations were formed is also informative. Of the groups for which the author has information regarding their date of origin, there is a lower probability of pacifist beliefs among groups formed later. Thirteen of 21, or 62%, of groups formed by 1917 give evidence of being pacifist at some point in their history. Twenty-four of 48, or 50%, of those groups formed by 1934 give evidence of pacifism at some point in their history. Of those groups formed after 1934, 11 of 54, or 20%, give evidence of pacifism at some point in their history. Three of 15, or 20% of those groups for which the author has no evidence of their date of origin, have been pacifist at some point in their history.

An analysis of the type of pacifism adhered to by these denominations suggests a strong reliance on the original statement formulated by the Assemblies of God in 1917. Few Pentecostal groups have been absolute pacifists or give evidence of presently being absolute pacifist. Six groups use the term conscientious objection to describe their pacifism. Two of these qualify their pacifism in such a way that noncombatant service is allowed. Four appear to be absolute pacifists.

While the largest part of the text of the prototype pacifist statement by the Assemblies of God was devoted to scriptural texts which support the pacifism, the portion which gave interpretation to those scriptures contained what appeared to be a formula for later statements. This formula included (1) an affirmation of the legitimacy and loyalty to government, (2) an absolute pacifist ethic based in scripture, and (3) a qualification of the absolute pacifism to allow noncombatant service in war. The Assemblies of God statement affirmed legitimacy of government and loyalty to the government in the following:

> While recognizing Human Government as of Divine ordination and affirming our unswerving loyalty to the government of the United States, nevertheless we are constrained to define our position with reference to the taking of human life.
> ...Therefore we, as a body of Christians, while purposing to fulfill all the obligations of loyal citizenship, are nevertheless constrained to declare we cannot conscientiously participate in war...[25]

At least seven groups followed with statements of loyalty. The following are examples of loyalty statements:

- ready to serve the government...
- willingness to serve...
- serve country in any capacity except bear arms...
- willing to serve in any capacity outside taking up arms...
- serve country in any capacity except bear arms...
- loyalty to U.S. ...
- obedience to laws, but not in war...
- obey government...except in its use of armed force...
- duty to obey...laws that do not contradict God's word...
- affirm civil government...[26]

The Assemblies of God gave a qualification of absolute pacifism in stating that their position was defined "with reference to the taking of human life," and "the actual destruction of human life."[27] At least 14 groups gave qualifications which allowed noncombatant services in war. Most of these used the term noncombatant service or against combatant service. The following are examples of this type of qualification which would be interpreted as noncombatant service:

- not take up arms...
- not take up arms in war...
- not to take up any weapon of destruction to slay another...
- against combatant service in war, armed insurrection property destruction, aiding...destruction of human life...
- [against] actual destruction of human lives, but will serve in any capacity outside of taking up arms if required to do so...28

Thus, the rhetoric of pacifism was moderated in the option of noncombatant service.

Evidences of Pentecostal Pacifism In Various Countries

Because Pentecostalism made its first advances into Europe at the time of the European War, evidence of Pentecostal pacifism is found in Europe. It seems to be lacking in other areas where conscription was not an issue, or where at the time of the arrival of the Pentecostal Movement, conscription was not an issue.

Pacifism took hold in English Pentecostal circles early in World War I. Although there were notable detractors, it was as strong there as in America, and shows signs of outliving the American variety. The Elim Foursquare Gospel Church adopted a pacifist position which they held until World War II when it was rejected.[29] The Apostolic Church (South Wales) takes a position as "absolutely opposed to war," yet allows members to choose whether to participate.[30]

There were expressions of pacifism in Pentecostal groups in other parts of Europe during World War I. The *Weekly Evangel* in 1917, noted the international character of the Pentecostals' belief in pacifism:

> From the very beginning, the movement has been characterized by Quaker principles. The laws of the Kingdom, laid down by our elder brother, Jesus Christ, in His Sermon on the Mount, have been unqualifiedly adopted, consequently the movement has found itself opposed to the spilling of the blood of any man, or of offering resistance to any aggression. Every branch of the movement, whether in the United States, Canada, Great Britain or Germany, has held to this principle. When the war first broke out in August of 1914, our Pentecostal brethren in Germany found themselves in a peculiar position. Some of those who were called to the colors responded, but many were court marshalled and shot because they heartily subscribed to the principles of non-resistance. Great Britain has been more humane. Some of our British brethren have been given noncombatant service, and none have been shot down because of their faith.[31]

Hollenweger notes that the Swiss Pentecostal Mission has taken an absolute stand against war "as an expression of violence, which is emotional and not godly." However, he also notes that "there are no conscientious objectors in the Swiss Pentecostal Movement."[32]

During the Revolution, the Russian Pentecostals maintained a position of pacifism. This changed during a time of extreme persecution from Soviet authorities in 1927 to a position of "admonishing members to participate in military service."[33] This was no small matter with the Assemblies of God in the United States who were sponsoring this work, and they seriously considered withdrawing support over this issue.[34] However, pacifism can still be found among the Pentecostals in Russia today.[35]

Footnotes

1. Significantly, in the face of wholesale refusal by constituents (in World War II) to abide by these beliefs, many groups have retained rather strong pacific statements.
2. David W. Faupel, *The American Pentecostal Movement: A Bibliographic Essay* (Wilmore, Kentucky: Asbury Theological Seminary, 1972), p. 44-45.
3. *Weekly Evangel*, August 4, 1917, p. 6.
4. *Ibid.*
5. *Ibid.*; Piepkorn, *Profiles*, pp. 113-115, 119-120, 131-134, 140-141, 130-131, 143; *Constitution and Bylaws: The Filipino Assemblies of the First Born, Incorporated* (Delano, California: 1954, pamphlet).
6. Piepkorn, *Profiles*, pp. 145, 156, 136-137, 134.
7. Charles W. Conn, *A History of the Church of God* (Cleveland: Pathway Press, 1977), p. 151.
8. Vinson Synan, *The Old Time Power* (Franklin Springs, Ga.: Advocate Press, 1973), p. 210. George H. Paul, "The Religious Frontier in Oklahoma: Dan T. Muse and the Pentecostal Holiness Church," (Ph.D. dissertation: University of Oklahoma, 1965), pp. 141-143, notes there were a number of "ardent pacifists" in that church.
9. Piepkorn, *Profiles*, pp. 102, 112.
10. *Ibid.*
11. Walter J. Hollenweger, "Black Pentecostal Concept," *Concept Journal*, special issue no. 30 (June 1970): 27-28; Hollenweger believes this group to be twice the size of the Assemblies of God which is considered by many to be the largest Pentecostal group.
12. *Ibid.*, p. 33; Everett LeRoy Moore, "Handbook of Pentecostal Denominations in the United States," (M. A. Thesis, Pasadena College, 1954), p. 181; citing *Church of God in Christ Yearbook* (Memphis: Church of God in Christ Publishing House, 1951), pp. 88-89. This statement quotes words used by Lincoln to lead the North in a war to free slaves.
13. Piepkorn, *Profiles*, 178-191; Charles W. Conn, *A History of the Church of God* (Cleveland: Pathway Press, 1977), p. 151; Vinson Synan, *The Old Time Power* (Franklin Springs, Ga.: Advocate Press, 1973), p. 210. George H. Paul, "The Religious Frontier in Oklahoma: Dan T. Muse and the Pentecostal Holiness Church," (Ph.D. dissertation: University of Oklahoma, 1965), pp. 141-143,

The Extent of Pentecostal Pacifism 35

14. Hollenweger, *Pentecostals*, pp. 45-46; citing *Triumph the Church and Kingdom of God in Christ, Junior Guide and Easy Lessons* (combined), (n.p.: n.d.), p. 15.
15. Piepkorn, *Profiles*, pp. 36-37.
16. Piepkorn, *Profiles*, pp. 202-203.
17. *Manual: United Pentecostal Church International* (Hazlewood, Mo.: United Pentecostal Church International, 1974), p. 27.
18. Piepkorn, *Profiles*, p. 199; also Moore, pp. 246-247.
19. *Ibid.*, pp. 199-200.
20. *Ibid.*, p. 210-211.
21. *Ibid.*, p. 200.
22. See Piepkorn, *Profiles*.
23. *Ibid.*, p. 100.
24. Piepkorn, *Profiles*, pp. 105-106, 119, 122, 126, 128, 130, 132, 143, 145, 181, 190; *Articles of Faith: Church of God of the Apostolic Faith, Inc.* (Tulsa: n.p., 1951), n.p.; *General Constitution and By-Laws: The Pentecostal Church of God of America* (Joplin, Mo. n.p., 1975), p. 22; John Thomas Nichol, *Pentecostalism* (New York: Harper & Row Publisher, 1966), p. 142-144; *Constitution and By-Laws: The Filipino Assemblies of the First-Born, Incorporated* (Delano, Calif.: n.p., 1954), p. 11; The following have similar views on war: Church of God of the Mountain Assembly, Inc. (1907), Churches of God of the Original Mountain Assembly, Inc. (1946), Calvary Pentecostal Church, Inc. (1932), Church of God of the Apostolic Faith (1914), Pentecostal Church of God of America (1922), International Pentecostal Assemblies (1936), The Pentecostal Fire-Baptized Holiness Church (1918), Emmanuel Holiness Church (1953), General Assembly of the Church of the First-born, Church of God of the Union Assembly (1920), Filipino Assemblies of the First-born (1933), Olzabal Latin-American Council of Churches, Inc. (1936), Christ Faith Mission (1939), Full Gospel Church Association (1952), and (original) Church of God, Inc.; The Church of God (1957 reformation, Cleveland) allows the individual to decide. See also Moore, pp. 85, 98, 149, 181, 228, 234, 246-247, 274, 286, 300.
25. *Weekly Evangel*, Ag. 4, 1917, p.6.
26. Piepkorn, *Profiles*.
27. *Weekly Evangel*, August 4, 1917, p.6.
28. Piepkorn, *Profiles*.
29. Bryan R. Wilson, *Sects and Society: A Sociological Study of Three Religious Groups in Britain* (Westport, Conn.: Greenwood Press, 1961), pp. 88-89).
30. *The Apostolic Church: Its Principles and Practices* (Gradford, Great Britain: Apostolic Publications, 1961), p. 147.

31. "The Pentecostal Movement and the Conscription Law," *Weekly Evangel*, August 4, 1917, p. 6.

32. Walter J. Hollenweger, *The Pentecostals: The Charismatic Movement in the Churches* (Minneapolis: Augsburg Publishing House, 1974), p. 401.

33. Christel Lane, *Christian Religion in the Soviet Union: A Sociological Study* (London: George Allen & Unwin, 1978), p. 176.

34. Paul B. Peterson to Noel Perkin, September 21, 1928; Paul B. Peterson to Noel Perkin, June 13, 1929; Paul B. Peterson to Noel Perkin, July 12, 1929; Memo. "REEM," by the General Council of the Assemblies of God, Inc., April 30, 1935; These letters furnished by Jeff Henderson, Assemblies of God Graduate School, Springfield, Mo.: See also Steve Durasoff, *The Russian Protestants: Evangelicals in the Soviet Union, 1944-1964* (Cranbury, N. J.: Associated University Presses, Inc., 1969), pp. 81-82.

35. Lane, pp. 183-184; Hollenweger, *Pentecostals*, p. 281; Lawrence Klippenstein, "Exercising a Free Conscience: The Conscientious Objectors of the Soviet Union and the German Democratic Republic", *Religion in Communist Lands*, Vol. 13, No. 3, Winter, 1985, pp. 284-285.

CHAPTER III

MAJOR PERSONALITIES IN THE DEVELOPMENT OF PACIFISM IN PENTECOSTAL CIRCLES

Any attempt to trace the pacific tendencies of Pentecostals in the past is problematic. First, pacifism is not a key ingredient in the self-understanding of these groups and their historians.[1] Second, documentation for the beliefs of Pentecostals who did not belong to the largest groups is difficult to obtain since many were not broadly published. Because of the limited availability of source material, there is some unevenness in the treatment of these early leaders.

The Logic of the Early Leaders' Pacifism in the Pentecostal Movement

The widespread adoption of pacifist statements throughout the early Pentecostal Movement suggests that pacifism was no mere appendage to their ethical beliefs. Pacifism was integrated into the fabric of their world view. Chief among the elements of that world view was intense millennial expectations coupled with anti-nationalistic allegiances. Millennial expectations placed hope for a just society outside of the present configuration of power in this world. This fueled an anti-nationalistic sentiment as did their missionary zeal and redemptive identification with other peoples around the world.[2] They found war repulsive because of its obvious incongruence with the missionary impulse. They did not identify strongly with nationalistic goals because they perceived that, given their low social status, those goals were never framed with the early Pentecostals in mind. These elements of their world view, coupled with a restorationist view of the church, provided a matrix of which pacifism was an integral part.

A number of early Pentecostal leaders, as well as one forerunner to the movement, gave explicit formulation to their views on war and peace. These views are of interest because they shed light on the early Pentecostal world view and are integrated into a fabric of faith and life.

John Alexander Dowie

Many today find it difficult to empathize with those who hailed John Alexander Dowie as Elijah, the Restorer, or John the Baptist. However there may be some irony in the fact that Dowie was an important forerunner to the Pentecostal Movement.[3] Dowie's pacifism was related to his world view, especially his impulse to restorationism and missionary zeal. It is doubtful if Dowie's social status was comparable to many early Pentecostal leaders, but the status of those to whom he made his greatest appeal must have been lower class.[4] It may even be that he served as an example of lower class status mobility as a religious entrepreneur.

John Alexander Dowie was born in Edinburgh, Scotland, and studied at Edinburgh University from 1869-1871. In 1872 he became the pastor of a Congregational church in a suburb of Sydney, Australia. Dowie gained notoriety in 1876 by introducing the practice of faith healing in his ministry.[5] By 1883 he broke with the Congregational church in Australia. Coming to the U.S., he established Zion's Tabernacle in Chicago.[6] Soon he unveiled his dream to build Zion City, Illinois, and chose a site north of Chicago. Under his leadership, and with control of 6,500 acres of farmland bordering Lake Michigan, Zion City became a reality and "flourished as a theocracy from 1901 to 1906." In its heyday it was home for 10,000 people who intended to escape the evils of their age. Phillip Cook notes that the "inhabitants of this city were definitely planning to practice the precepts of the Master."[7]

Before Dowie established his utopia at Zion, he distinguished himself by his opposition to such evils as liquor, medicine, eating pork, smoking and secret societies. It was in building Zion that he planned to deal with these and broader social and economic problems. Here was to be found the remedy for the "evils in labor, industry, finance, and politics."[8] This would come about by applying the teachings of Jesus directly to society. Dowie was outspoken in his beliefs concerning racism. He advocated miscegenation, saying that it was "essential to restoring the primitive strength of man."[9]

Dowie was no traditionalist, and in every area of his thought one can see development over time. No one should doubt Dowie's millennial utopianism previous to his building Zion, yet it seems that his radical views were only enhanced by his initial success in building Zion. His apparent belief in polygamy may be a case in point. It surfaced only after some time in Zion.[10] His belief in pacifism was not fully developed at the time of the Spanish-American War. At that time, he supported war to bring an end to racial injustice.[11] His belief in pacifism did not become apparent until 1901, when it began to intensify. Dowie reflected a larger societal context in which the American public was largely disinterested in matters of foreign affairs until the late 1890s.[12] It is not surprising that Dowie framed his views on war in contrast to public sentiments; he was a prophet. Given the time frame of this development in Dowie's thinking, it also seems probable that Dowie was influenced in his ideas on pacifism by Arthur Sydney Booth-Clibborn, who will be treated in the next section. For this reason, Dowie's developing pacifism will be treated in the next section of this chapter along with Booth-Clibborn.

There may have been other forces influencing Dowie's thinking in this regard. Dowie had yet to incorporate a view of war and peace into his continually evolving view of the church and society by the time of the Spanish-American War. It may be that the war was a catalyst that in time crystallized his thinking. In January 1898, months before the United States declared war on Spain, he criticized President McKinley for his hesitancy to intervene and bring protection to the *reconcentrados* in Cuba. He noted:

> I am no advocate for war, but there are worse things than war. There is the dishonor of a dishonorable peace, and I shall never for the sake of being afraid of a fight with the devil enter into a dishonorable peace of any kind. (Applause.) And if I had

been President of the United States eighteen months ago and more, the guns of the warships would have been booming upon Havana fortress telling them they could not murder with Impunity.[13]

Dowie reflected the sentiments of the working class who gave him applause, many of whom viewed the insurrection in Cuba as "another hemispheric nation striving for an American style freedom."[14] Dowie also reflected similar statements among the press and clergy.[15]

By 1900, Dowie published teachings which chastised nations of Europe for their large standing armies and penchant for warfare. None of the comments went as far as pacifism, but they were advocating Christian peacemaking.[16]

It is doubtful that Dowie met the Booth-Clibborns before 1900, but on his European trip that year he visited extensively with them in London and Paris.[17] During this same time he wrote an editorial from London setting forth the beliefs of the Christian Catholic Church in Zion.[18] It was also the time of the Anglo-Boer War in South Africa, a time in which Arthur Sydney Booth-Clibborn had begun to speak out against that particular war as a pacifist. Within a short time Booth-Clibborn would write a book, *Blood Against Blood*, in which he condemned the war and argued a Christian view of pacifism.[19]

Arthur Sydney Booth-Clibborn

Booth-Clibborn was born in a family with a 250-year ancestry of Quakers. As a young man, he became a Quaker minister.[20] Having been schooled in France and Germany, he was fluent in French and German. For this reason, the Salvation Army invited him to go as a missionary to France and Switzerland in 1881.[21] There he met and married Catherine (Katie) Booth, daughter of the Salvation Army founder, William Booth.[22] Their experiences during this time prepared them to make a prophetic statement against war. As missionaries in Europe for the despised Salvation Army, they were often persecuted; on numerous occasions they spent time in jail for preaching the gospel and trying to help the poor. The Swiss government opposed them on both counts.[23] Catherine and Arthur Booth-Clibborn became involved in civil disobedience when they were not allowed to preach the gospel. Catherine won the affectionate title of the *Marachale* (field marshal) for her work which led to religious liberty for the Salvation Army in France and Switzerland.[24]

During the Anglo-Boer War, Arthur Booth-Clibborn was commissioner for the Salvation Army in Holland and Belgium. He was in a unique position as an Englishman to see through the propaganda both sides were using to promote their cause. The book he wrote used many classic Quaker arguments against war from scripture and reason. It also appealed to figures from church history who opposed war. The thesis of the book contrasted two kinds of bloodshedding: one carnal in war; the other spiritual in Christ and the martyrs. Carnal war and spiritual war (the latter for which the Salvation Army was named) were never to be confused. In many cases however, the church had defended the nation where it resided, mixing the two kinds of blood. This was the supreme confusion. Christianity was the only antidote to war. It was the blood of Christ against the blood of the bayonet. Booth-Clibborn argued, like the Quakers, that the loss of pacifism in the church occurred at the time of Constantine and was solely the result of the great apostasy. The greatest reforms in the church had advocated pacifism as a part of returning to New Testament Christianity.[25]

Booth-Clibborn also related his pacifism to his eschatology. He was in no sense given to optimism. Instead, he held to a premillennial pessimism, as presented in the following question and answer:

> But do you think war will be abolished by Christianity at its present rate of progress?
> No. But that has nothing to do with our individual duty. One of the most glorious and solemn parts of the programme of Christianity is that the King is soon coming to claim the Throne of the World.... We appear to be now well on into the Saturday Night of the World.[26]

Since Booth-Clibborn held that this was the time of the end, and the solution to wars would only come with the second advent of Christ, he had no desire to link arms with secular pacifists in the cause of peace. It was futile for Christians to impose their rules of conduct on the world. In like manner, he placed no hope in the working class opposition to war because he saw in it an inverse violence directed at the rich. After noting that the working classes "paid in blood and labor to support the war," while the upper classes profited from it, he said "this antiwar movement is thus a declaration of war in another form, -- war between the masses and the classes. It has nothing to do with Christianity."[27]

The Christian's place was to declare the insanity of war and participate in the war for converts. Carnal war was adverse to Christian missions, which were based on a love for all nations. How could one work to bring other nations to Christ, and then destroy them? War was the opposite of mission work. He stated:

> The worldling knows only one kind of brotherhood -- that in Adam. The Christian knows two, that in Adam and that in Christ. In war the worldling denies one kind of tie in killing his fellow-creature; the Christian denies two kinds -- he kills his fellow-creature and his fellow-Christian ... Besides, the former has ever a "field" (a battlefield) open to him which the latter has not; he can sacrifice his life as a missionary, and, if needs be, as a martyr, and "sow himself" thus a seed of righteousness and life-producing life rather than as a seed of sin and death-producing death, which every sacrifice of life on the carnal battlefield inevitably is![28]

Thus, Booth-Clibborn's pacifism was related to his eschatology, his awareness that wars were not fought in the interest of the poor, and his opposition to war as a contradiction to Christian missions.

The reasons why the Booth-Clibborns left the Salvation Army related to their contact with Dowie. Booth-Clibborn held hopes that General Booth would have been more disposed to pacifism.[29] Since this was not the case, he chastised the Salvation Army for having a Navy and Military League. This did not sit well with the General.[30] The time Booth-Clibborn left the Salvation Army coincided with the secession of a number of other sons and sons-in-law of the General over the General's authoritarian rule.[31] Finally, the Booth-Clibborns left the Salvation Army because of their involvement in a healing ministry. This also led them to meet with Dowie in London in 1900.[32]

When Dowie left for Europe in 1900, the newspapers asked him to write an editorial explaining the beliefs of the Christian Catholic Church. In the article, he included a statement written from London that would serve as a model introduction to statements on pacifism from which the Pentecostals would later frame their positions. It read:

> Zion loyally renders unto Caesar, whether he be President, Czar, Emperor, or King, that which belongs unto Caesar; and yet Zion absolutely refuses to recognize the right of Caesar to enter the domain of the conscience or to interfere with the actions of those who offend no righteous law, but live quiet, peaceable and good lives.[33]

Shortly before leaving for Europe, Dowie spoke to the student body at Zion College. He came closer to an absolute pacifism than ever before. He condemned capital punishment on the basis of the commandment, "Thou shalt not kill," and he called for using the "Sword of the Spirit," rather than shedding blood. In terms much like those of Booth-Clibborn, he contrasted warfare with Christ who shed his own blood that no other blood be shed. He condemned the United States for bloodshed in the Philippines, as well as the Boers and the British for their bloodshed. Like Booth-Clibborn, he was sad that England was sending out thousands to murder rather than to serve as missionaries. Still, he maintained a reservation that he would drop at a later time. He said:

> "I believe, therefore, that capital punishment is always wrong, and that war is always wrong, except it be a war for protection."[34]

He related this to missions in a poem:

> Along our ranks no sabres shine,
> No blood-red pennons wave;
> Our banners bear one single line:
> "Our mission is to save."[35]

Dowie related pacifism to his eschatology, by showing that if this was to be the ethic for the coming Kingdom, it should be taught now. He closed his speech with the following words:

> What a blessed day it will be when all "the kingdoms of the world is become the Kingdom of our Lord, and of His Christ." That is what we are looking for. That is what we have to preach. The day is coming when that shall be taught. Zion therefore stands for peace and not for war.[36]

Less than a year after Dowie met with the Booth-Clibborns in London in November, 1901, Arthur Booth-Clibborn wrote to Dowie asking to become a member of the Christian Catholic Church. He noted in a letter how his life had been "nine times attempted," but that he could "never... go out of (his) way to avoid death, or use carnal weapons." It took some adjustment for Booth-Clibborn to accept Dowie as Elijah. His resolution came in light of his millennial views.

> ... it could only be a Gigantic Error, or a Gigantic truth, filled with unspeakable solemnity, even though "Elijah was a man of like passions with ourselves." I take it that you come in the spirit and power of Elijah, and as the Herald of the Second Coming, the Baptist of the Millennial Dawn.[37]

Kate Booth-Clibborn could not agree with the "Elijah matter," and it would be some time before she joined with her husband; however Arthur's brother left the Salvation Army with him to join Dowie.[38] Dowie was elated at highly respected European leaders joining his movement. General Booth was understandably angered. From this time on, Dowie made his strongest statements on pacifism.

General Booth began to attack Dowie in the press, thus allowing Dowie an opportunity to solidify his views on pacifism and distinguish his church as superior to the Salvation Army. He did this in a sermon with a text from

Zechariah titled, "Not By an Army." The text was used to argue for pacifism and against using an army motif for the church. Dowie asked Percy Clibborn who was attending the service;

> Elder Clibborn, did you ever hear a sermon preached upon this text in a Salvation Army Corps, in which it was translated properly?
> Elder Clibborn -- "No, sir."
> General Overseer --But I will give it to you properly... O brother William Booth... the time has come for your army to disappear![39]

Dowie continued by arguing the ineffectual outcome of the Civil War, and that what was needed was a kingdom, not an army.

By July 1902, Arthur and Kate Booth-Clibborn were in Zion, and Dowie used the occasion to preach on two of their favorite themes: pacifism and women in the ministry. In a worship service Dowie invited Kate to speak. Dowie read the scripture from Matthew 5:

> The Revised Version says, "Blessed are the peacemakers for they shall be called sons of God." He paused when he read this and explained that he did not like the use of the word "sons" as well as the word "children." He favored giving woman an equal place in the ministry with man.[40]

He now preached as a pacifist.

> I do not hesitate to direct... every member of the Christian Catholic Church in Zion never to take a gun or shoot a man.(Applause.) If they force you into the army, you have to go. You can carry the gun, but you need not hit anybody. (Laughter and applause.) You can protest against going to war. You can say that you will not fire a shot that will kill. I do not think that there could be a more powerful protest than a man saying that he would not do it.[41]

He encouraged members if they were conscripted, to volunteer for medical duty.[42]

Over the next few months Dowie was outspoken in publishing and speaking against war, and linking his remarks to the coming "chaos" in the world that would lead to the "rapture."[43] He reiterated his belief that to fight in battle was a sin.[44]

In July 1902, Arthur and Catherine Booth-Clibborn were baptized by Dowie in Shiloh Tabernacle, in Zion, Il.[45] However, it was only months later when the Booth-Clibborns left the Chicago area to return to Europe. At Dowie's request, they also submitted their resignations from membership in the Christian Catholic Church.[46] It appears that Catherine clashed with Dowie over two matters. The first was Dowie's unmerciful attacks in the press against her father, General Booth.[47] Proclaiming Booth a liar and himself as God's prophet Elijah, Dowie warned of Booth's impending death should Booth fail to repent.[48] While Catherine also had differences with her father, which led her out of the Salvation Army, this public renunciation angered her. When she and Arthur left for Europe, she would only say that they "had had enough of Dowie".[49] She also failed to resolve the "Elijah matter" of Dowie's identitiy. It was apparently not until the following year that Dowie met with the Booth-Clibborns in Zurich, Switzerland, and effected reconciliation with them.[50]

By 1903, Dowie was condemning Roosevelt's work to build up the Navy. President Roosevelt spoke in Chicago Auditorium and told of his desire to build up the Navy. Although Dowie was far from poor, he saw that war placed the greatest burden on those with the least to gain from it.

Major Developers Of Pacifism

> What does war mean? ... What do these great navies mean? In the first place they mean terrible taxation, grinding oppression, and wholesale murder. The poor of all these lands have to labor and toil for the creation of these vast armies and navies, and for the paying of large sums of money to aristocratic officers who walk about in gold lace, and red and blue uniforms, and who are counted heroes because they know how to cut other men's throats.[51]

In this statement he was able to identify with the bulk of people in Zion, who remained poor in spite of coming to Zion and needed someone to blame for their continued poverty.

By 1904, Catherine Booth-Clibborn rejoined the Christian Catholic Church, along with her husband, as an elder of the church in Holland. She now submitted fully to Dowie as Elijah the Restorer.[52]

In that same year, Dowie spoke on "The Duty of Zion in Time of War," in response to the Russio-Japanese War. He was saddened that here was one more case where the "Christian" nations had set a poor example in their early contacts with Japan. He saw this war as turning into a world-wide conflict, and instructed Zion people to "...be killed rather than kill!...all who are under the Banner of Zion, you must not carry a sword, or a gun, or take part in the working of artillery, whether on sea or land."[53]

Again Dowie encouraged his followers to participate in the ambulance corps. He was careful to counsel them not to "give deadly drugs, or perform cruel operations," both of which ran counter to his belief in divine healing. Dowie was certain that this war would involve Zion people, and he began to encourage his closest followers, the Restoration Host, to learn how to tie up an artery; how to deal with men who can exercise no faith; who cannot cooperate with you in praying the Prayer of Faith. It is well to know how to staunch a deadly wound, and how to keep one from bleeding to death.[54]

Dowie argued for some kind of international police force, although he did not specify how this differed from an army, or what the relationship of Zion people would be to this group. He thought a police force would be necessary in order to preserve peace after this great war.[55]

In 1905, Dowie reiterated in strongest language that one could not participate in bloodshed in war and remain a member of the Christian Catholic Church.[56]

One cannot know how Dowie would have responded to World War I, which became the point at which Pentecostals had to interpret their views about war, because he was removed from leadership in the Christian Catholic Church in 1906 and died in 1907.[57] A number of early Pentecostal leaders came from Zion, which was for some time a center of Pentecostal activity. Although Dowie was not a Pentecostal, he did influence those early Pentecostal leaders who had been a part of his church in Zion.

Anton Darms, an apostle in the Christian Catholic Church in Zion, was still teaching pacifism in the *Leaves of Healing*, Dowie's magazine, in 1916.[58]

Booth-Clibborn became a Pentecostal and had a significant influence on Pentecostalism in teaching pacifism in the United States and Europe.[59] In 1915, the *Weekly Evangel* noted Booth-Clibborn's Pentecostal ministry in Germany, and advertised his book.

> The Pentecostal people, as a whole, are uncompromisingly opposed to war, having much the same spirit as the early

> Quakers. . . . Indeed, some have already urged us to arrange for a great peace council among the Pentecostal saints, to put ourselves on record as being opposed to war at home or abroad. . . . The Gospel Publishing House is now in possession of a powerful book entitled, *Blood Against Blood*, written by Arthur Booth-Clibborn, an English Pentecostal brother who has been the means of a glorious ministry in Germany before the opening of the war. . . . We recommend that you purchase it and become imbued with the spirit of its contents, in a complete opposition and protest against war and the shedding of blood.[60]

Thus, the name Booth-Clibborn became associated with pacifism in the Pentecostal Movement.

Charles Fox Parham

One of the earliest Pentecostal leaders was Charles Fox Parham.[61] Parham had been influenced early in his ministry by a Quaker family, the Thistlethwaites, and married a daughter, Sarah. Conversation with David Baker, Mrs. Thistlethwaite's father, encouraged major changes in Parham's doctrine. He now adopted the doctrine of total annihilation of the wicked. Anderson notes that:

> It was probably while under this holiness Quaker's influence that Parham also came to reject water baptism, to accept sanctification as a second act of grace, and to regard church membership as a matter of indifference.[62]

It is possible that his views on pacifism were formulated in like manner.

Much of Parham's teaching dealt with themes of eschatology. In bold apocalyptic terms, he painted the near future as a time of great distress leading to Christ's coming and the arrival of the millennium. This also influenced his ethic on war. At the time of World War I,

Rolland Romack, Parham's office editor and manager for his paper, the *Apostolic Faith*, was inducted into the service. Romack asked for exemption from combative service. However it was not granted. Parham explained:

> For over twenty years we have seen these present wars coming... All this time we have taught that true Christians must not fight for "he that taketh the sword shall perish with the sword..." It is hard for those who sincerely believe that we are nearing the end of this age and the shedding of blood to be of no avail, to fight for the perpetuation of these nations, which we know will fall as the Gentile age will close and the millennium come, when the nations of the world shall become the kingdom of our Lord and Savior, Jesus Christ.[63]

Almost every biblical passage had some eschatological significance, and the prophetic could even be affirmed in non-biblical sources. Parham referred to James 5, and an apocryphal vision attributed to George Washington, and stated:

> Prophecy states that near the time of the end the nation will become lifted up and forget God and spread itself abroad in power and self-glory and sorely oppress the laborers in their hire. For these things God will bring the nation to a close and the whole body of the eagle will be burned, as Washington, in his vision of the close of this nation's history, saw the cities laid waste from coast to coast. This will surely come true in the struggle between capital and labor.[64]

Parham did not hesitate to chastise the churches for their alliance with the state and opposition to the poor. After warning that "the Judge is standing at the door," Parham reflected:

> The past order of civilization was upheld by the power of nationalism, which in turn was upheld by the spirit of patriotism, which divided the peoples of the world by geographical boundaries, over which each fought the other until they turned the world into shamble [sic]. The ruling power of this old order has always been the rich, who exploited the

masses for profit or drove them in masse to war, to perpetuate their misrule. The principle teachers of patriotism maintaining nationalism were the churches, who have lost their spiritual power and been forsaken of God. Thus, on the side of the old order in the coming struggle, will be arrayed the governments, the rich, and the churches, and whatever forces they can drive or patriotically inspire to fight for them. On the other hand the new order that rises out of the sea of humanity knows no national boundaries, believing in the universal brotherhood of mankind and the establishment of the teachings of Jesus Christ as a foundation for all laws, whether political or social.[65]

Parham saw World War I as a transition to a new age.

> The opening of the war, in 1914, marked the descent of the Devil from the Heavens... It is now the opening of the midnight hour, when Jesus says to his servants (real consecrated Christians), "Go ye out into the highways and hedges, and compel them to come in."[66]

The work of the Christian in the closing times was primarily missions.

In 1914, Parham preached a sermon titled, "War! War! War!," in Zion City condemning the nations of Europe for commercial and imperialistic motivations for the war. He warned of coming destruction of the United States, and ended with a contrast between the call to arms and the call to be a missionary, reminiscent of Booth-Clibborn:

> Recapitulation: War! War! War!--What For? To murder a fellow-creature! To receive therefore even less than thirty pieces of silver, and perhaps live to receive the plaudits and honor of a more cowardly country and imbecile nation; for that nation is imbecile which retains its existence through the struggling exploits of war. We hang our heads in shame to see Christian nations and individuals yield themselves to the embrace of the Moloch-God, Patriotism, whose principle doctrine was honor (?), there to have consumed in the death struggle the feeling of philanthropy and humanity; spending millions to build the fires for the consummation of these virtues,

while the cause of Christ languishes, heaven loses, hell opens her jaws, and so-called Christian nations feed (by war) to satisfy her gluttonous appetite...

Yet while thousands of men will volunteer and suffer the hardships and privations of an earthly war for glory, few, indeed, will volunteer and endure the slightest privations for the Master's kingdom and eternal glory.[67]

In summary, Parham consistently related his pacific views to his millennial eschatology, his identification with the poor, and his zeal for missions.

Frank Bartleman

Frank Bartleman may have gained his pacifist beliefs from his Quaker mother.[68] Bartleman was a Holiness minister in Los Angeles, who grew to some prominence in the revival at Azusa Street in 1906 and through his continuous writing and travels.

The Azusa Street mission catered to the lower class as the following "prophecy" given by a poor woman, Mary Galmond, in the *Apostolic Faith* (Azusa Street), illustrates:

> Labor Against Capital
>
> The Lord says, "The time is coming when the poor will be oppressed and the Christians can neither buy nor sell, unless they have 'the mark of the beast.'" Then He says: "The time will come when the poor man will say that he has nothing to eat and work will be shut down. And the rich man will go and buy up all the sugar, tea, coffee, etc... and hold it in his store, and we cannot get it unless we have the mark of the beast."
>
> "That is going to cause the poor man to go to these places and break in to get food. This will cause the rich man to come out with his gun to make war with the laboring man. They will cause blood to be spilt in the street as it never was before." I saw blood ankle deep, and they were holding to the horses' bridles with the right hand and cutting and slashing right and

Major Developers Of Pacifism 55

> left with their swords. And the Lord said the blood would be in the streets like an outpouring rain from heaven. He says all these unions are bringing the sword to their own head, to cut their own heads off. (I had never heard of unions before the Lord showed me this and I asked my husband what "labor against capital" meant.)[69]

Many in this lower socio-economic group interpreted their social position and the present wars apocalyptically. They perceived that whatever the outcome of this conflict for world domination, they would still be the losers.

Frank Bartleman conceived of socialism playing an important role in the coming apocalyptic conflict. Shortly after World War I, he published a tract, *Christian Citizenship*, in which he contrasted two conflicting systems, with the Christian caught between. The two systems were socialism and the apostate church. He identified the apostate church with the "autocratic, ruling, capitalistic classes." He noted that "this is world politics. What place has a Christian in it? It is all corruption and hypocrisy, hopelessly fallen." To him, "The Christian is a man without a country... He renounces his earthly citizenship... when converted as surely as one renounces his citizenship in the United States should he swear allegiance to a foreign country."[70] He was sure that war had compromised the church:

> One of the greatest crimes of the late war was that of robbing the church of her sacred calling and "pilgrim" role, turning her aside from the saving of souls, to plunge her into the vortex of world politics and patriotism, with all its fallen prejudices and preferences, avarices, cruelties, hates and murder... The church has no place to flaunt flags of national preference. God's grace and gospel are international. Christ died for all men.[71]

What should the Christian do in time of war?

> Gov't is squarely up against God in its demands on Christians during war time. And Christians are squarely up against the question whether they shall obey God or Man.... Should those in authority forbid the preaching or practicing of the Gospel, which Gospel forbids to the Christian the exercise of war, there is but one thing for him to do. He must obey God.[72]

As early as 1914, Bartleman had been spreading the word of peace in Pentecostal circles in Europe. From 1912 to 1914, he took a trip to visit Pentecostal missions in Europe, including Russia, Germany, and England. He met Pentecostal people in all these places and was not convinced that Germany warranted destruction. It is probable that he spent time with Arthur Booth-Clibborn while in Europe. Bartleman was incensed at what he perceived to be a mercenary motive behind much of the patriotism in London. He spoke at the Pentecostal Home of Sister Cantell. He recalled that "most of my messages were against the war spirit."[73] At the Central Pentecostal Mission in London he met resistance:

> The Lord gave me a strong message against the war spirit in Christians. The leader said if he were a young man he would enlist himself. They were opening their meetings with a "War Hymn." The Conscription Act had not yet passed. My message dropped like a bomb in the camp. But some thanked me for it later, especially some of the missionary student young men, members of the P.M.U....
> I spoke at Pastor Saxby's Mission Sunday morning. Here God gave me a strong message against the war spirit also. But it was very differently received. The leader thanked me warmly. He had come into Pentecost, with his congregation, from the Baptist Church. The other mission was really Church of England. They had never severed their connection fully with the State Church System.[74]

Pastor Saxby, who gave a favorable response to Bartleman, was the pastor of a young man named Donald

Gee.[75] Gee became a conscientious objector to World War I, and continued to promote pacifism longer than any other Pentecostal leader.

Bartleman would have nothing of the English propaganda running throughout the United States press. He wrote an article for the *Weekly Evangel* in 1915 titled, "The European War." He argued compellingly concerning the hypocrisy of the allies and brutalities of both sides. Condemning the injustice done to the lower classes in England, he said, "God is done with the class system in England." He condemned the whole affair as madness.[76]

In a similar article in 1915, Bartleman called for repentance, noting that the motives behind the war were mercenary:

> This war is not a holy war. It is the result of pride, greed, jealousy, hatred, hypocrisy, etc... The whole thing is a game of chess, with the nations as the players. Kings and leaders, capitalists, are the chess men. They play their nations as the stake. Rulers for their private purse, bankers and financiers of the world for gain, munition manufacturers and provision merchants, all work together in this game. Flesh and blood of the common people, soldiers, are either forced or hired to do the fighting. Rev. 18:13.[77]

Bartleman, son of a German immigrant, compared England and Germany, but painted Germany in fairer shades.

> The sins of Germany are many. But she has accumulated what she has by hard labor. She is in a wonderful state of organism and cultivation. Such a nation cannot be destroyed. England must follow her example. Instead of preserves for the sporting of the rich, fox hunting, cricket, etc., she must plant potato patches. Poverty stalks abroad all over in England. Her populace is in a most precarious condition.[78]

He condemned America not only for supplying munitions to England for profit, but for a history of terrible oppression regarding American Indians.[79]

Bartleman published the tract, *Present Day Conditions*, which was also published in the *Word and Witness* in June 1915. Present events were interpreted in the light of prophecy and judgment. He condemned America for greed and hypocrisy in the *Lusitania* affair. He grieved the devastation to missions brought by the war.[80] The Gospel Publishing House circulated the tract until the passage of the Espionage Act and its amendment, the Sedition Act, in 1917 and 1918 respectively. These laws made it treasonous to talk of peace.[81] Because anything considered pro-German was seditious, the editor of the *Christian Evangel* called upon readers to destroy Bartleman's tract, noting that:

> While this tract was merely aimed at sin high or low, and while the things said would be understood in times of peace, that it was entirely too radical for war times.[82]

This retraction by the leaders of the Assemblies of God led to Bartleman's publication of another tract after the war titled, *War and the Christian*. He felt that "the Pentecostal people had failed to stand by the Lord." Bartleman believed he had been under government surveillance during the war.

> One could not preach "love your enemies," or even "pray for them" honestly. To do so brought down a storm upon our heads. To be a Christian meant to be denominated "pro-German." Spies haunted every little Pentecostal meeting.[83]

Bartleman may have been the most radical in his approach to pacifism, yet he was not alone. Like others, he framed his pacifism in terms of his millennial es-

Major Developers Of Pacifism 59

chatology, his identification with the poor, and his internationalism fueled by missions.

Bartleman and Booth-Clibborn had an effect on Pentecostal leaders, especially in England. Among these was Donald Gee who would be the chairman of the Assemblies of God in Britain from 1948 until 1966. Gee was the last of the early Pentecostal leaders who believed in pacifism. Bartleman and Booth-Clibborn affected John and Howard Carter who also became leaders in the Assemblies of God in Britain. Stanley Frodsham, who played a key role in the early years of the Assemblies of God in the United States, both in the formulation of its creed in 1916, and his work with the *Pentecostal Evangel* until 1948, was similarly influenced.

Stanley H. Frodsham

Stanley Frodsham had a great deal of influence on the Assemblies of God, and helped formulate its creed in 1916. He was closely associated with the *Pentecostal Evangel* from 1916 to 1948.[84] Little of his opinion on pacifism seems to be documented, but Carl O'Guin believes that he was one of the more absolutist of the pacifists in the beginning who helped formulate the Assemblies of God position regarding war.[85] Frodsham was an Englishman who came into the Pentecostal Movement in 1908.[86]

Frodsham wrote on the subject of "Our Heavenly Citizenship" in an article in the *Word and Witness* in 1915. He proposed an other-worldly view, which would influence an ethic in times of war. He called for going beyond nationalism and patriotism, recognizing one's heavenly citizenship. He said,

> National pride, like every other form of pride, is an abomination in the sight of God. And pride of race must be one of the all things that pass away when one becomes a new creature in Christ Jesus."[87]

This affected his views on war as seen in the following:

> When seen from the heavenly viewpoint, how the present conflict is illumined. The policy of our God is plainly declared in the Word, "Peace on earth, good will toward men. "The nations who have drawn the sword to kill those of the same blood in other nations, for God "hath made of one blood all nations of men," are not merely fighting against one another, but with their policy of "War on earth and ill will toward men," they are without knowing it, again fulfilling the Scripture, "The kings of the earth set themselves and the rulers take counsel together, against the Lord and against His anointed." Is any child of God going to side with these belligerent kings? Will he not rather side with the Prince of Peace under whose banner of love he has chosen to serve?[88]

The article ended with an apocalyptic description of how God and the saints would triumph.[89] To Frodsham, the issue was one of being distinct from the world, in terms which were clearly eschatological.

Donald Gee (1891-1966)

Donald Gee, a British Pentecostal, came into the Pentecostal Movement in 1905 during the Welch Revival. For a number of years he was pastor of the Assemblies of God in Edinburgh. From 1934 to 1944, he was vice-chairman of the Assemblies of God in Britain, and from 1948 until 1966 he was chairman. Until 1964, he was in charge of the Assemblies of God Bible School in London.[90] As a spokesperson for Pentecostals and their distinctive views, he also tried to encourage Pentecostals to foster ecumenical relationships. He had a keen sense of ethical duty. In a Bible study on Acts 2 he noted: "We may find excellent reasons for rejecting the idea of communism, but those professing to be filled with the Spirit of Christ have the responsibility of showing a realistic alternative."[91] Gee seems to be the last Pentecostal leader of consequence to write in favor of pacifism. Gee was influenced in World War I by both Booth-Clibborn and Bartleman to become a conscientious objector. In his history of the Pentecostal Movement in Britain, *Wind and Flame*, Gee notes Booth-Clibborn's influence on Pentecostals:

> The whole nation, but especially the soldiers, seemed to be singing Tipperary at that time, and so Mr. Booth-Clibborn, true to Salvation Army methods, wrote the following sacred words to the worldling's tune. They were appreciated alike by Christian fellows in the Forces, and those suffering for conscience sake.
>
> It's a straight way that leads to glory,
> It's the way of the Cross;
> But it shines evermore before me,
> While I'm "counting all but dross"!
> Farewell, sin and sorrow,
> Goodbye, anxious care;
> It's a long, long way that leads to glory,
> But my heart's right there![92]

During World War I, the Assembly in Harringay, where Gee was a member, "let it be known that, as followers of Christ, its members could not participate in war and bloodshed."[93] This was simultaneous with Bartleman's visit to the Harringay church.[94] Gee filed conscientious objector status and gained exemption from military service to do "work of national importance" in agriculture.[95] Gee looked back on the experience as important in his development as a leader:

> The severe spiritual strain and stress this involved, including not only the fiery trial at the tribunal, but later the months and years of continual obloquy and petty persecution, meant a growth in character and conviction that would have come much more slowly under peaceful circumstances.[96]

Gee became a spokesman for pacifism in 1930 in a two-part article that ran in the *Pentecostal Evangel* in the United States. The article was prefaced with what came to be a prophetic insight, that the present generation was being reared without teaching on the issues of war, and that they will come to the time when war would break out and make a decision for which they were unprepared. He lamented the woeful record of the church as a whole in World War I in following Christ. Instead the church gave way to patriotism. He felt that the church's inconsistency in this matter had a great deal to do with the indifference of the general public to the church. In his opinion:

> However passionately patriotism may overwhelm everything else in time of war, the world certainly expects the Christian church to take a stand against war, and it is deeply disappointed at heart when that stand is not taken, however much it may persecute for the time the "conscientious objector."[97]

He argued that the Old Testament provided no justification for the Christian to go to war as:

> Its history comprises "times of ignorance" at which God winked (Acts 17:30); its spiritual dynamic was a law written on tables of stone, and enforced by heavy physical penalties on every hand (e.g., Leviticus 26, etc.); the very bringing in with Christ of a New Covenant of which the keynote is the word "better" (Heb. 8:5, etc.) was a proof of its temporary character.[98]

Major Developers Of Pacifism

In contrast, Gee wrote: "The teaching of Jesus is almost too familiar to need restating."[99] The dilemma came over the issue of being subject to the governing authorities on the basis of Romans 13. Gee was absolute that one must be subject, except where there is a conflict between God's laws and the law of man:

> Then the only answer for the Christian is contained in the immortal words of Peter, "We ought to obey God rather than men." Acts 5:29. Conscientious Objection then becomes the only possible course, however serious the consequences. The Bible puts clear before us the magnificent example of Daniel and the three Hebrews. Daniel 3 and 6. He who said "Render unto Caesar the things that are Caesar's" also said, "But unto God the things that are God's." The two are to be combined to the last possible limit, but when further combination of allegiance becomes impossible--then God must come first. The Christian's true citizenship is in heaven, Phil. 3:20.[100]

Gee then outlined three possible alternatives to the Christian faced with the choice of what to do in time of war: (1) noncombatant to actual killing, (2) no military participation, but willing to do work of national importance, and (3) the extremist who rejects both noncombatant status and work of national importance (a position Gee found impossible due to the degree that each individual participates in society whether voluntarily or not). He stressed the importance of allowing the individual to decide before God what he should do, but the options seemed limited to the three previously stated.[101]

Gee was speaking from the kind of experience he wished to avert in the future:

> The writer has observed as a solemn fact that those of our Pentecostal brethren who took a strongly patriotic attitude in the last war have mostly gone backward in spiritual power and influence ever since, while those who put Christ and His Word

before all have advanced by divine grace to positions of spiritual leadership. It could hardly be otherwise.¹⁰²

Ten years later, with England's entry into World War II, Gee published an article titled "Conscientious Objection," in the *Redemption Tidings* which was subsequently carried in the *Pentecostal Evangel*. The essence of the article was a plea for consistency by the conscientious objector in all areas of life. The conscientious objector should not take a job making armaments or airplanes. "Forestry, the growing of food, the maintenance of essential public services, are the type of occupation that need involve no defilement of conscience."¹⁰³ The article ended with a plea for understanding by the conscientious objector for those who do not share his views. It was a classic expression by one who was known for his ability to state his position clearly and at the same time maintain an attitude of respect and fair mindedness toward those with whom he disagreed.

> The purest conscientious objection carries with it the broadest tolerance for the sincere convictions of others, and finds its spiritual fellowship not in common agreement upon some creed, but in common loyalty to the truth as each one has found it in Christ.¹⁰⁴

Howard Carter

Howard Carter is included in this chapter because of his stand as a conscientious objector during World War I, and the fact that he became a leader in the Assemblies of God in Britain, serving on the Executive Presbytery for a number of years. The nature of his pacifism can be seen in his actual experience. He applied for conscientious objector status which was granted, conditional

Major Developers Of Pacifism 65

upon undertaking medical service. He said he was prepared to do this work provided that any men he nursed back to health were not returned to the fighting line.[105] This was denied, and he almost received a ministerial exemption, but his newly formed Pentecostal congregation was not a part of an existing denomination and as such was not recognized by the government. He was sentenced to prison, serving nine months in Wormwood Scrubbs Prison in London, and later at Dartmoor Prison. This was a time of earnest biblical study for Howard Carter in which he developed what was to become the principle teaching on spiritual gifts used by many Pentecostals following him. His brother, John, received better treatment and was given exemption from military duty to milk cows.[106]

Footnotes

1. Of three recent Pentecostal histories written by Assemblies of God historians, only Menzies mentions the subject, *Anointed to Serve: The story of the Assemblies of God* (Springfield, Mo.: Gospel Publishing House, 1971), pp. 326-328; Klaude Kendrick, *The Promise Fulfilled: A History of the Modern Pentecostal Movement* (Springfield, Mo.: Gospel Publishing House, 1961); Carl Brumback, *Suddenly From Heaven: A History of the Assemblies of God* (Springfield, Mo.: Gospel Publishing House, 1961). John Thomas Nichol, *Pentecostalism* (New York: Harper and Row, 1966), p. 144, mentions pacifism as exceptional to the movement as a whole, in the case of the International Pentecostal Assemblies; Walter J. Hollenweger, Pentecostals, pp. 26, 36, 51, 59, 118, 193, 200, 232-235, 280, 400-401, deals with the issue; this is likely due to his outlook as one related

closely to the World Council of Churches; Nils Bloch-Hoell, *The Pentecostal Movement: Its Origin, Development and Distinctive Character* (Oslo: Universitetsforlaget; London: Allen and Unwin; and New York: Humanities Press, 1964), does not deal with the issue. A nonpentecostal, Robert Mapes Anderson, *Vision of the Disinherited* (New York: Oxford University Press, 1979), pp. 198-224, deals extensively with the subject. Conversation with Chaplain Waugh, head of the Chaplains Department for the Assemblies of God in 1981 (September 1981, Springfield, Mo.) showed he was unaware that there had been any change in the position of the Assemblies of God on the subject of participation in war: this despite the fact that Menzies in his history notes under the heading of "Military Service," that the Assemblies of God early articulated a pacifist position, and that they "no longer officially affirmed a pacifist position." The situation is changing at the present. Since my thesis (North American Baptist Seminary, 1982) on the subject and a subsequent paper presented at the Society for Pentecostal Studies in Cleveland, Tennesee, Roger Robbins has published, "A Chronology of Peace: Attitudes Toward War and Peace in the Assemblies of God: 1914-1918," in *Pneuma: The Journal of the Society for Pentecostal Studies:* Spring 1984; pp. 3-25. Cecil Mel Robeck has published, *Witness to Pentecost: The Life of Frank Bartleman*, (N.Y.: Garland Publishing Co., 1985) which does a superb job of placing Bartleman's pacifism in context. Edith L. Blumhofer has written "The Christian Catholic Apostolic Church and the Apostolic Faith: A Study in the 1906 Pentecostal Revival," in *Charismatic Experience in History*, (Peabody, Mass.: Hendrickson Publishers, 1985) pp. 126-146, which connects the work of Parham and Zion, Ill. Dwight J. Wilson, "Pacifism," in: Dictionary of Pentecostal and Charismatic Movements, Stanley M. Burgess, Gary B. McGee, and Patrick H. Alexander, eds. (Grand Rapids, Mi.: Zondervan Publishing House, 1988) pp. 658-660.

2. The connection between speaking in tongues and missionary endeavor did not escape the early Pentecostalists. Some went to mission fields fully expecting to speak the foreign language by supernatural gifts.

3. Carl Brumback, *Suddenly From Heaven* (Springfield: Mo., Gospel Publishing House, 1961), pp. 72-73; Walter J. Hollenweger, *Handbuch der Pfingstbewgung* (Geneva: duplicated, 1965/67, 02a.02.047), pp. 459-60; Edith L. Blumhofer, "The Christian Catholic Apostolic Church and the Apostolic Faith: A Study in the 1906 Pentecostal Revival," in: Cecil M. Robeck, Jr., ed., *Charismatic Experiences in History* (Peabody, Ma.: Hendrickson Publishers, 1985), pp. 126-146.

Major Developers Of Pacifism 67

4. Philip Lee Cook, "Zion City, Illinois: Twentieth Century Utopia," (Ph.D. Thesis, University of Colorado, 1965), pp. 2, 9, 23, 124-125, 205, 247; *Leaves of Healing* (XII, March 21, 1903), pp. 684-5.

5. Robert S. Fogarty, *Dictionary of Communal and Utopian History*, s.v. "Dowie, John Alexander," (Westport, Conn.:Greenwood Press, 1980); In 1882 Dowie built a healing tabernacle in Melbourne.

6. *Ibid*.

7. Philip Lee Cook, "Zion City, Illinois: Twentieth Century Utopia," (Ph.D. Thesis, University of Colorado, 1965), pp. 2, 9.

8. *Ibid*., pp. 23, 247; citing *Leaves of Healing*, (XII, March 21, 1903) pp. 684-685.

9. John Alexander Dowie, *A Voice from Zion: Sermons and Addresses by the Rev. John Alexander Dowie*, vol. 5. (Chicago: Zion Printing and Publishing House, 1902), p. 30.

10. Arthur Newcomb, *Dowie: Anointed of the Lord* (N.Y.: Century Co., 1930), pp. 337-338; *Leaves* (Vol.XVII, 1905), pp. 173-175; *Leaves* (Vol.XVIII, 1905) p. 440.

11. Cook, p. 249; citing *Leaves* (IV. Feb. 12, 1898), p. 316.

12. Vincent P. DeSantis, *The Shaping of Modern America: 1877-1916* (Notre Dame, Ind.: Forum Press, 1981), pp. 115, 121.

13. *Leaves* (IV. 1900), p. 316.

14. Augustus Cerillo, Jr., in Ronald A. Wells, *The Wars of America: Christian Views* (Grand Rapids, Mich.: Wm. B. Eerdmans Publishing Co., 1981), p. 103.

15. *Ibid*.

16. *Leaves* (VII, 1900), p. 749; Inclusion of a date within this text suggests this was a republication of an 1894 sermon.

17. *Leaves* (X, 1902), p. 470.

18. *Leaves* (VIII, 1901), pp. 66-68.

19. Arthur Sydney Booth-Clibborn, *Blood Against Blood* (N.Y.: Charles C. Cook, 1914, 3rd ed.) There is no date for the original edition. I have placed the date between mid-1900 and early 1902; based on the fighting of the Anglo-Boer War and internal evidence in the book; 55-56.

20. *Ibid*., pp. 166-176; His ancestry included two military men who were converted to Quakerism. Colonel David Barkley and John Clibborn, ancestors of Booth-Clibborn, became Quakers in the same year (1655-6). John Clibborn was converted under the preaching of Thomas Lowe, who had also influenced William Penn. David Barclay's son, Robert, became a "Leading Quaker theologian." He traveled "in gospel service with George Fox and William Penn."

21. *Ibid.*, p. 175; At this time he stated that he "could never forego any of the essential truths of Quakerism, and entered the work on that understanding."
22. Thus he, like other sons-in-law of Booth, took the name of Booth.
23. Richard Collier, *The General Next to God* (New York: E. P. Dutton, 1965), pp. 161-163; In 1883 the Swiss government outlawed the Salvation Army. "Kate's reaction was automatic: She would test the power of the decree by disobeying it." Arrested at a public meeting, she spent twelve days in Neuchatel's cold medieval gaol. For a time the Salvationists were reduced to meeting in secret in Switzerland "like old time covenanters, gathering in pine-forests or blacksmith's forges, often to frustrate the police as early as five a.m." A. S. Booth-Clibborn met the same treatment. He and twelve others were "gaoled for holding an all-night meeting of prayer in a private house." In 1889, "Clibborn was dragged from his own hall, spent a memorable night in Geneva Gaol along with a thief and a prostitute; outside Clibborn's cell, gendarmes kept up a ribald non-stop chorus of Hallelujahs. Next morning a handsome gendarme, twirling his moustache, looked wantonly at the girl and remarked: 'How well you go together, you three--a thief, a prostitute and Clibborn. *Ah, c'est tout a fait ca.*' To Clibborn it was as if William Booth had pinned a medal on his tunic."
24. *The Marachale, They Endured* (London: Marshall, Morgan and Scott, Ltd., n.d.).
25. Booth-Clibborn, *Blood Against Blood*, pp. 24, 29, 36, 49-50, 55-57.
26. *Ibid.*, pp. 123-4.
27. *Ibid.*, pp. 125-6, 139.
28. *Ibid.*, p. 132.
29. Merl Eugene Curti, *Peace or War: The American Struggle 1636-1936* (N.Y.: Garland Publishing, 1972), p. 113; notes that the General had charged his followers to "teach men better manners than to go cutting one another's throats for their own base purposes."
30. Booth-Clibborn, *Blood Against Blood*, p. 175; Here seems to be a veiled reference to the disagreement between Booth-Clibborn and the General: "Mrs. Booth felt at the time considerably drawn towards those views,... It is my deep conviction that had she been alive during the last decade and face to face with its great military developments, and of threatening conscription in England, she would have agreed with the main lines of the book, and also with the definite stand taken by her eldest daughter Catherine, my dear wife, on this question at the time of the Anglo-Dutch War."

Major Developers Of Pacifism 69

31. Sallie Chesham, *Born to Battle* (Chicago: Rand McNally and Co., 1965), pp. 95, 110; The General decided to reshuffle all his leaders to various countries, in what seemed to be a move to prevent them from getting too powerful. This did not set well with most and there was a refusal, termed as "insubordination," which led to a division in the Salvation Army in 1896.
32. P. W. Wilson, *General Evangeline Booth of the Salvation Army* (N.Y.: Charles Scribners Sons, 1948), pp. 138-9; links all three factors: (1) pacifism, (2) divine healing and association with Dowie, and (3) insubordination, with Booth-Clibborn's departure.
33. *Leaves* (VIII, 1901), pp. 66-68.
34. *Ibid.*, p. 212.
35. *Ibid.*, p. 213.
36. *Ibid.*
37. *Leaves* (X, 1902), pp. 571-2.
38. *Ibid.*
39. *Leaves* (XI, 1902), p. 331.
40. *Blood Against Blood*, 171-2; argues strongly for women in ministry; *Leaves* (XI, 1902), p. 600.
41. *Ibid.*, p. 601.
42. *Ibid.*, pp. 601, 771.
43. *Ibid.*, p. 724.
44. *Ibid.*, p. 770.
45. *Leaves* (XI, 1902), p. 476.
46. "Booth's Children Quit Zion," *Chicago Inter-Ocean*, Nov. 4, 1902; "Couple Feels Dowie's Wrath," *Chicago American*, Nov. 4, 1902.
47. "Elijah Dowie In Great Fury, Denounces Gen. Booth as a Liar," *Detroit Journal*, Nov. 17, 1902.
48. *Ibid.*; "Hurls Curse at Booth," *Chicago Chronicle*, Nov. 17, 1902.
49. "Had Enough of Dowie," *Topeka, KS., State Journal*, Nov. 7, 1902; "Roundly Denounces Dowie: Mrs. Booth-Clibborn Accuses the Zion Overseer of Lying," Chicago Chronicle, Dec. 22, 1902.
50. *Leaves* (XV, 1904) pp. 355-6.
51. *Leaves* (XII, 1903), p. 783.
52. *Leaves* (XV, 1904), pp. 335-6.
53. *Leaves* (XVI, 1905), pp. 149-151.
54. *Ibid.*
55. *Ibid.*, p. 186.
56. *Leaves* (XVII, 1905), p. 687.
57. *Leaves* (XVIII, 1906), p. 437.
58. *Leaves* (XXXVII, 1917), pp. 436-440; (XXXIX,1917?) n.p.
59. Brumback, *Suddenly From Heaven*, 64-46, 339; Notes Eric Booth-Clibborn died as a young man shortly after reaching the

mission field, a missionary for the Assemblies of God. W. C. Booth-Clibborn was a charter member of the General Council of the Assemblies of God (*General Council Minutes*: Assemblies of God, 1914, 13). William E. Booth-Clibborn was one of the leaders of the "first Southern Bible Conference" sponsored by the Pentecostal Assemblies of the World in 1922, and later was one of the founders of the Apostolic Churches of Jesus Christ, a oneness Pentecostal group (later to merge with the United Pentecostal Church); William E. Booth-Clibborn, *A Call to Dust and Ashes* (St. Paul: Author, n.d.); Arthur L. Clanton, *A History of Oneness Organizations* (Hazlewood, Mo.: Pentecostal Publishing House, 1970), pp. 18, 30, 33; Frank K. Ewart, *The Phenomenon of Pentecost* (St. Louis: Pentecostal Publishing House, 1947), p. 54.

60. "Pentecostal Saints Opposed to War," *Weekly Evangel* (June 19, 1915), p. 1; *Weekly Evangel* (July 10, 1915).

61. Klaude Kendrick, *The Promise Fulfilled: A History of the Modern Pentecostal Movement* (Springfield, Mo.: Gospel Publishing House, 1961), pp. 37, 50-52.

62. Robert Mapes Anderson, *Vision of the Disinherited* (N.Y.: Oxford University Press, 1979), p. 49.

63. Sarah T. Parham, *The Life of Charles F. Parham* (Joplin, Mo.: Tri-State Printing Co., 1930), pp. 273-4.

64. *Ibid.*; see also Charles F. Parham, *The Everlasting Gospel* (n.p., 1911, n.p., n.d., reprint ed.), pp. preface, 19-21, 26-30.

65. Charles F. Parham, *Everlasting Gospel*, pp. 27-28.

66. *Ibid.*, pp. 28, 489, 60; Parham notes the necessity of premillennialism and the hopelessness of peace conferences (much like Booth-Clibborn).

67. *Ibid.*, pp. 78-83.

68. Cecil M. Robeck, Jr., *Witness to Pentecost: The Life of Frank Bartleman* (N.Y.: Garland Publishing, Inc., 1985).

69. "Testimony and Prophecy," *Apostolic Faith* (Los Angeles, Oct., n.d.) 2 pages.

70. Frank Bartleman, *Christian Citizenship* (Los Angeles: Author, n.d.) 2 pages.

71. *Ibid.*

72. *Ibid.*

73. Frank Bartleman, *Two Years Mission Work in Europe Just Before the War 1912-1914*; 47, 54-55; Margaret Cantel was the daughter of one of Dowie's elders. Her husband was Dowie's overseer in Britain; see D.W. Cartwright in, Dictionary of Pentecostal and Charismatic Movements (Grand Rapids, Mi,: Zondervan, 1988) p. 107.

Major Developers Of Pacifism 71

74. *Ibid.*; The one mission was trying to be a renewal movement within the Church of England. It was led by Rector A. A. Boddy Who predictably followed the Church of England which was unashamedly pro-war. Ray Abrams, *Preachers Present Arms* (Scottdale, Pa.: Herald Press, 1969, revised), p. 31, documents the role of the Church of England in the War.

75. John Carter, *Donald Gee: Pentecostal Statesman* (Nottingham: Assemblies of God Publishing House, 1975), p. 16.

76. Frank Bartleman, "The European War," *Weekly Evangel* (July 10, 1915), p. 3.

77. Frank Bartleman, "What Will the Harvest Be?" *Weekly Evangel* (Aug. 7, 1915), p. 1.

78. *Ibid.*; C. M. Robeck, "Frank Bartleman," in Dictorary of Pentecostal and Charismatic Movements (Grand Rapids, Mi.: 1988) pp. 50-51, notes Bartleman's German ancestry.

79. *Ibid.*, pp. 1-2.

80. Frank Bartleman, "Present Day Conditions," *Word and Witness* (Je. 1915), p. 5.

81. Abrams, *Preachers Present Arms*, 66, 128; notes that during this time, "While some were showing the Sermon on the Mount to be a great war document, ministers were being jailed for quoting texts from it. . .One group circulated a pamphlet containing the Sermon on the Mount without comment and the Department of Justice warned against its distribution."

82. "Destroy This Tract," *Christian Evangel* (Aug. 24, 1918), p. 4.

83. Frank Bartleman, *War and the Christian* (n.p., n.d.), p. 4.

84. Menzies, *Anointed To Serve*, pp. 118, 133; he was editor from 1921-1948.

85. Phone conversation with Carl O'Guin, Jan. 16, 1982.

86. Menzies, p. 132. Frodsham may have been influenced by the pacifism of Bartleman and Booth-Clibborn.

87. Stanley H. Frodsham, "Our Heavenly Citizenship," *Word and Witness*, Oct. 1915, p. 3.

88. *Ibid.*

89. *Ibid.*

90. Hollenweger, *Pentecostals*, p. 208.

91. *Ibid.*, pp. 208-213.

92. Donald Gee, *Wind and Flame*, revised, enlarged, and re-entitled (Croydon: Heath Press Ltd., 1967), p. 102.

93. Howard Carter, *Donald Gee: Pentecostal Statesman*, pp. 17-18.

94. Frank Bartleman, *Two Years Mission Work in Europe*, pp. 54-55.

95. Carter, *Donald Gee*, p. 18.

96. *Ibid.*
97. Donald Gee, "War, the Bible, and the Christian," *Pentecostal Evangel*, Nov. 8, 1930, p. 6.
98. *Ibid.*
99. *Ibid.*, p. 7.
100. Donald Gee, "War, the Bible and the Christian," part II, *Pentecostal Evangel*, Nov. 8, 1930, p. 6.
101. *Ibid.*, p. 3.
102. *Ibid.*
103. Donald Gee, "The Conscientious Objector," *Pentecostal Evangel*, May 4, 1940, p. 4.
104. *Ibid.*, p. 5.
105. John Carter, *Howard Carter: Man of the Spirit* (Nottingham: Assemblies of God Publishing House, n.d.), p. 39.
106. *Ibid.*

CHAPTER IV

MAJOR PERSONALITIES WHO MODERATED PACIFISM IN PENTECOSTAL CIRCLES

MODERATES

Eudorus N. Bell (d. 1923)

E. N. Bell, unlike other leaders, reflected less absolutism in pacifism due to his training in non-holiness circles. His education also distinguished him from other Pentecostal leaders.[1] As a result, he spoke from a different social status than the rest of the early Pentecostal leadership. The radical outlook of the uneducated leadership, common to the movement, was tempered in Bell.

Bell was compelled to pacifism for two reasons. He was a part of a movement that was largely pacifist and the biblical case for pacifism was attractive. This pacifism, however, was combined with a healthy dose of patriotism, as well as an awareness of the dangers to the young movement from an extremely antagonistic government.

E. N. Bell was a significant leader of the Assemblies of God through its initial years of formation. Bell was the first chairman of the General Council in 1914, and then later from 1920 until his death in 1923. In 1910 he became the editor of the *Apostolic Faith* magazine (Malvern, Arkansas). He was also editor of the *Christian Evangel* from 1918-1919.[2]

It is difficult to assess the thinking of Bell with respect to pacifism because he edited the *Christian Evangel* shortly after entry of the United States into World War I and the passage of the Espionage and Sedition Acts. While it is apparent that he was not as absolute as others in his pacifism, it is not clear to what degree this was influenced by the tremendous curtailment of the rights of dissent in the United States at that time.

In January 1918, six months after passage of the Espionage Act, Bell wrote a warning to the preachers of the Assemblies of God. The article noted that:

> The General Council has always stood for law and order. So at our last Council Meeting we took a strong stand for Loyalty to our Government and the President and to the Flag. Let all note this and be duly warned.
> Since then we have noted with sorrow that a half dozen preachers have been arrested and put in jail by U.S. Marshals for opposing this war, failing to register in the draft, and such things. While some of these are of the Pentecostal faith, so far as we know none of them are affiliated with the General Council of the Assemblies of God. But knowing some are not trained in wartime laws, we feel like dropping a note of warning.[3]

Bell warned Pentecostals that "many utterances allowable in times of Peace may be Treasonable in Times of War, such as the present."[4] Bell's position became common to Pentecostals. This fit well with their pessimistic premillennial eschatology which recognized that wars were inevitable, and that the Christian's response was not to try to stop war, but rather not to participate in the actual killing. Bell noted:

> It is one things [sic] to be in our own faith opposed personally to taking human life, even in war, but quite another thing to preach against our Government going to war. It is unlawful to do so. It is none of our business to push our faith as to war on others or on the Government.[5]

Finally, the article gives telling evidence of the effect of the government's exemption on ministers who may have been more radical had they been drafted. Bell continued: "Preachers who are excused from war ... are under double obligation to show their gratitude to God and the Flag for such religious liberty and prove this by extra service and sacrifices to the good of mankind, to the Government and to God."[6]

Later the same month, Bell encouraged Pentecostals to give to the Red Cross and buy Liberty Bonds. This was a definite compromise in the eyes of English Pentecostals who were going to prison rather than work in hospitals for the treatment of soldiers who would go back to battle. Nevertheless, Bell was forthright in stating:

> Anybody who can buy bonds at all may own a Liberty Bond, whether saint or sinner. All citizens who can will do a patriotic deed in buying a Liberty Bond. The man who buys a postage stamp and mails a letter contributes to the war as same as [sic] the one who buys a bond. If we appreciate the religious freedom we have under the stars and stripes, we will not want to bow our necks to the Prussian yoke or the Kaiser. God save our Country![7]

In February 1918, Bell wrote an article that betrayed the tremendous sensitivity that Pentecostals had regarding these issues. He noted how their consciences were disturbed over being asked to kill for their country, and support those who did the killing with taxes. Bell argued that if Jesus paid taxes and worried little how the Roman Government spent them, the Pentecostal should do likewise. While Bell argued biblically, he was not unaffected by the government's propaganda efforts at justifying the war. So he again spoke in bold patriotic terms:

> Let us hope for every oppressor our country has to kill it may save a thousand others from slavery to the Kaiser, and while the country is trying to save the world from physical, mental and commercial slavery, let us save the souls from slavery to sin and bondage to Satan.[8]

Bell reiterated the same kinds of argument in June 1918 commending all who had purchased Loyalty Bonds. Bell quoted the Apostle Paul's admonition to submit to authority:

> He did not want the work of the Lord to get into any disrepute through the spirit of anti-Christ, which is the spirit of anarchy, that is abroad in many hearts these days. Any spirit of disloyalty is certainly not of Christ, for his own blessed Word shows from beginning to end that "the powers that be are ordained of God," and if we resist them we "resist God."[9]

Bell gave no credibility to other Pentecostals who would see the occasion when civil disobedience was necessary and right. By now, the Sedition Act had passed and freedom of speech was totally withdrawn. For obvious reasons, Bell called upon Pentecostals to destroy the tract by Frank Bartleman titled, "Present Day Conditions."[10]

Clearly, Bell's views about the legitimacy of the state were different from other Pentecostals and he drew a distinction between their views on pacifism. It came to clearest expression when Bell argued from the legitimacy of local law enforcement to the work of a soldier. The article was a series of questions and answers of which the following was one:

> Would it be murder for a child of God to go to war and shoot Men as do other soldiers?
> Ans. Our faith leaves this with the conscience of each man. We have never opposed the going to war of our members whose conscience allowed them to go. But everyone must keep personal hatred out of his heart. The sheriff who hangs the criminal as commanded by law need have no hatred in his heart, and he is not a murderer when he obeys his country in executing just punishment on the criminal Hun.[11]

Bell opened the way for Pentecostals to justify going to war to kill. It was difficult to convince the average layman to practice non-cooperation with the government in a call to arms, with Bell's arguments ringing in the background.

Ernest S. Williams

Because of the times of his ministry, E. S. Williams served as a bridge between the earlier stronger statements on pacifism, and the later rejection of pacifism by the American Assemblies of God. Williams was the General Superintendent of the General Council from 1919 to 1948.[12] The movement began to change from a revivalist movement to a fully-organized denomination during this time. Williams' time of office and his writing on pacifism correspond to that of Donald Gee, the British Pentecostal leader.

In 1936, Williams published an article that gives evidence of radical elements in the movement which the leadership felt a need to reorient. The article also gives evidence to the reshaping of eschatology that was necessary for the Pentecostals when World War I did not bring the end of the world. It seems that this move in eschatology was to become tied to the American experience as was the Pentecostal phenomenon itself. The article recounts the events of the past four years, when the President dealt with the problems of the Depression. Williams noted the great political and religious freedoms in the United States. He regretted, on biblical grounds, hearing remarks of disrespect against those in authority. He encouraged subjection to government, which was legitimized on the basis of Romans 13. Pentecostals were very rapidly becoming a part of the emerging status quo. The radical edge, in this case, the Depression Era poor who might grumble against the system, was being blunted by a change in social status afforded, at least in part, by denominational success and recognition of ministerial status. Williams' teaching was more reserved than earlier Pentecostal leaders. The movement was consolidating, putting all traces of fanaticism in its past.[13] The movement was not given to otherworldly views on nationalism and patriotism at this time. Williams warned:

> Some have felt that their allegiance to God forbids their saluting the national flag or respecting the Government of the Nation. We feel sorry for those who sincerely feel thus. They are suffering from being wrongly taught. While "our citizenship is in heaven" and "we seek a country" those are blessings of hope to be realized when the present age is past and we enter "the everlasting kingdom," our eternal home. But we are also citizens of our native land and subject to its laws. Let us recognize our relationship both to "the everlasting kingdom" which we fondly hope to enter, and to the present civil order of which we are also a part.[14]

With the potential for the United States entry into World War II as a backdrop, Williams wrote an article on "The Conscientious Objector," in the *Pentecostal Evangel*. He argued against what he called the "full-fledged pacifist" position which was an absolute position against war, and therefore non-cooperative with the government. Rather, he called for the Assemblies of God to be classified as a group of "conscientious objectors." In this manner, they could pledge to "assist the Government in time of war in every way morally possible."[15] The implication of the article was a call for noncombatants who work as medics, or conscientious objectors working in medical units or reconstruction efforts. He recommended that churches and individuals adopt the practice of the Broadway Tabernacle in New York which

> provided a statement for its members which, after it is signed, is preserved with the church records to show it to have been the free act of its members. It is quoted here and it would be well for other churches which believe it is not according to the spirit of Christ to take human life, to adopt a statement which meets its approval. There are other societies which have arranged statements for their followers, but the writer prefers that of the Broadway Tabernacle to others which he has read. It reads as follows:
> I have quietly considered what I would do if my nation should again be drawn into war.
> I am not taking a pledge, because I do not know what I would when the heat of the war mood is upon the country. But in a mood of calm consideration I do today declare that I cannot reconcile the way of Christ with the practice of war.
> I do therefore set down my name to be kept in the records of my church, so that it will be for me a reminder if war should come; and will be a solemn declaration to those who hold to this conviction in time of war that I believe them to be right and I do desire with my whole mind and heart that I shall be among those who keep to this belief.

> I set down my name to make concrete my present thought upon the question of war, and declare my purpose to think and talk with others about it, that my belief in the way of Christ shall become operative in this and in other questions which now confuse our thought and action.[16]

Williams was able to affirm this position for those who had conscientious beliefs on the matter. This is a significant example of the movement's allowance for diversity and of Williams' ability to write in a conciliatory manner. Williams did not believe that it was murder for a soldier to take life in time of war. A month later in a question and answer column he was asked:

> Were one soldier to kill another in battle would it be held against him?
> I should not like to consider it as murder, as some claim, since the same God who said to Israel, "Thou shalt not kill," at times commanded Israel to engage in wars. However, in this dispensation we are followers of the Lord Jesus, "the Prince of peace," who has said, "they that take the sword shall perish by the sword." Christians should ever be loyal and helpful to their Government, but it would be well for them to request noncombatant service in time of war.[17]

Such arguments were to moderate Pentecostal pacifism and paved the way for its replacement with other views. They were definitely contrary to the pacifism espoused by the early Pentecostals, who held it to be a great evil to take the life of another.

By 1961, pacifism, as well as noncombatant status, was nearly forgotten in the Assemblies of God. In that year the question was put to Williams in another way:

> Can we support the military program of our country and be in the will of God?
> I believe this must be left up to the individual conscience. The Assemblies of God is officially on record as being willing

to do anything for our government in time of war that does not require the bearing of arms. But many of our Spirit-filled young men have refrained from claiming this exemption, nor do they seem to feel they did wrong by taking up arms to defend our country.[18]

This was followed by a question as to the propriety of worship of God on Sunday morning and playing volleyball in the afternoon. Williams answered in the negative, as this would transgress the Scripture, "Remember the sabbath day to keep it holy."[19] Hollenweger notes the irony:

> It is true that Williams leaves open the question of whether military service can be reconciled with the Christian conscience. Everyone must decide this according to his own conscience. But that one should not play volleyball on a Sunday afternoon is quite clear to him; it is a compromise with the world.[20]

The writings of Williams reflected a considerable change within the Assemblies of God in America during this time.

Lycurgus Reuben Lynch

Little is known of the biographical details of Reuben Lynch, except that he was a "Bible teacher in Central Bible Institute," in Springfield, Missouri, the headquarters for the Assemblies of God. It appears he taught there sometime during the mid 1930s to the mid 1940s.

Lynch wrote a pamphlet titled, *Can a Christian Bear Arms?* It is undated, but probably was written between 1935 and 1945. Although the pamphlet dealt with a number of related arguments against the Christian going to war, some of them classic, it did have a central focus.

Lynch argued that God's involvement, directly and by sanction, in warfare in the Old Testament teaches that God uses war "in the exercise of His moral government over nations." In war God would punish evil nations. But the key question Lynch wanted to answer was, "Should a spirit-filled Christian engage in the taking of human life in the name of war?" For Lynch, war was a result of human government. Human government was initiated by the Naochian Covenant (Gen. 9). God instituted human government after the flood to "hold in check evil forces until the fulfillment of His plan."[21] War was the organized force of one government against another. According to James 4, wars were caused by lust. Lynch had no illusions about the righteousness of war.

Lynch postulated there are two covenants presently in effect. Unbelievers are under the Noachian Covenant which provides for government. Believers are under the New Covenant. According to Lynch, only those conditions of the Naochian Covenant which preceded it or those reaffirmed in the New Testament are binding on the Christian. There was one facet of that covenant not reaffirmed in the New Testament for the Christian believer: "It is the one which is concerned with the highest prerogative of human government--that of taking human life in the name of the State. But this is still in force with the unsaved."[22] From his reading of the Bible, Lynch distinguished two classes of "ministers," both corresponding to the appropriate covenant. Under the New Covenant there are "ministers in spiritual things," such as preachers and teachers, while under the Naochian Covenant there are policemen, magistrates, and executioners. Each has a function as a servant of God, in the appropriate sphere. Lynch argued, it is not murder when an executioner does his job, avenging the blood of one slain unjustly. However, the Christian must never fill this role. This he based on the fact that Jesus refused to cast the first stone at the adulteress who under law deserved to die. Lynch is to be commended for his ability to see where his thinking would lead. Like the Anabaptists, the pacifist would always be called to spell out clearly his view of the state and the Christian's role in leading a state. Thus it has been common for Anabaptists to reject the magistracy as an appropriate place for the Christian to serve.

Lynch ended the pamphlet by stating an alternative to participation in killing during wartime. Based on the principle that "the Son of Man is not come to destroy men's lives but to save them," he called on Christians to participate in anything constructive which could save lives. He argued:

> Any kind of service that aims directly at the conservation of human life is Christian. Under this heading we classify almost all branches of noncombatant service, except, of course, the manufacture of munitions, etc., which hardly comes under this classification. Any kind of service that aims directly at the destruction of human life is anti-christian.... So if you ask me whether I can take human life in time of war, I must answer, But for my Lord, I could; -- until He fail me, I cannot. (Lu. 6:46; Heb. 13:5, 6.)[23]

It is impossible to say what influence Reuben Lynch or his pamphlet had on Assemblies of God young men training for the ministry at the time of World War II. During World War II, few Assemblies of God young men chose either noncombatant status or absolute pacifism. The Assemblies of God counseled men during World War I to comply with the government in noncombatant work in the military. The fact is, however, that lines are difficult to maintain once one has agreed to be a part of the military. It is possible that compliance with the military in noncombatant roles led to softening the stand on pacifism and eventual loss of that belief.

DETRACTORS

Not all early Pentecostal leaders agreed with the pacifist position. Two observations relating to these people are in order: first, they tended to come from non-Wesleyan backgrounds; and second they tended to be those, who for reasons of evangelism, wished to make inroads of ministry into the military. In the latter case, a strong evangelistic ministry to servicemen needed to address two questions. First, how could an absolute pacifist gain the good graces of the military authorities in order to gain access to the soldiers? Second, what does one tell soldiers once they are converted? Are they to leave the military? It would seem from a pragmatic point of view, that the answer to these questions might determine the success of ministry to servicemen. If the answer is that the soldier who is born again should stay in the military, this immediately destroys some of the arguments that would keep other Christians from serving in the armed forces.

Alexander A. Boddy and Cecil Polhill in Britain

Alexander Boddy and Cecil Polhill became leaders in the Pentecostal Missionary Union before World War I. The Pentecostal Missionary Union (PMU) was a missionary arm of the church, but not a new denomination. Alexander Boddy remained in the Anglican Church as a priest while working with the PMU. Through the revival in his parish, All Saints in Sunderland, a number of leading Pentecostals came into the movement including Stanley Frodsham. Boddy held no pacific sentiments, but was predictably in line with the Anglican Church in support of England in World War I. Cecil Polhill was one of the landed gentry and a "squire of Howbury Hall, who had been at Eton and [was] one of the 'Cambridge Seven' (a group which also included C. T. Studd)."[24] As testimony to the fact of the great difference between Polhill and the other Pentecostals in social status, Hollenweger notes:

> It made a great impression on the Pentecostals that he, a wealthy upper-class landed proprietor, should preach in their meetings and should share his hymnbook at street meetings with a servant girl.[25]

Polhill was an unlikely candidate for the kind of pacifism held by Bartleman and Parham, which included a critique of the war based on its use for increasing the wealth of the wealthy.

In December 1914, the *Christian Evangel* printed a series of editorials reprinted from *Confidence*, a magazine published in England by Boddy. The editorials provided a Christian justification for British involvement in World War I. The first editorial, authorship unknown, reflected Boddy's sentiments. It is likely that it was written on the occasion of Frank Bartleman's visit to Britain. Bartleman recorded resistance from certain Pentecostal leaders there, but experienced some success with convincing other young men belonging to the PMU. One of these may have been Stanley Frodsham who later wrote as a pacifist.

The editorial admitted that Britain deserved chastening, which was probably a response to Bartleman's fierce attack on the motives of Britain for entering the war. The editorial proceeded from there to justify British involvement, as one who protects the weak from a bully. The editor wrote:

> Awful as war is, it would be worse to stand by, and make no effort to protect the weak. Better to fall as a nation than to stand by and see those crushed whom we have promised to help. We can pray for our dear sailors and soldiers with a clear conscience in God's sight. We will pray for victory.[26]

Cecil Polhill was quoted in the article from a letter he wrote to Boddy. Polhill noted his work along with the "Bros. Booth-Clibborn" in visiting camps of German prisoners in England, to preach and circulate tracts. Polhill's comments were guarded and tended toward peacemaking. Following the editorial, there was the text of an address by a non-Pentecostal speaker at Keswick justifying involvement in the war. The address appears to have been written by W. Graham Scroggie, who took a position with which most Pentecostal leaders disagreed.

> I am quite sympathetic with those who are genuinely exercised as to whether or not a Christian man should go to war; but let us remember that the laws which govern the Church of God as such, don't govern the Nations of the earth as such. It is not the Church of God that has gone to war, but the British Empire, and both are fulfilling divine purposes, though those purposes are not the same. Let us also remember that every Christian is a citizen of some State: shares in the benefits of that state, and has obligations to discharge in relation to it. When a man becomes a Christian, he does not shake off the state, neither is he lifted out of it. . .
> The work of the Church of God as such, is to preach the Gospel, to make Christ known as Savior and Lord, both by word and life. But in addition to that, it is the duty of Christians

as citizens to suppress intemperance, to wage war against immorality, to protect children, to provide for the aged and hopeless, and to prevent wanton cruelty to animals.[27]

The article was rebutted by Burt McCafferty the following month in the *Christian Evangel*. William Burton McCafferty was a charter member of the Assemblies of God.[28] McCafferty took an absolute pacifist stand, and based his entire teaching on the Scriptures. McCafferty's central argument was a Scripture which meant a great deal to Pentecostals who had a very literal understanding of the spirit world. In McCafferty's words:

> We are not contending with flesh and blood. Our warfare is waged against the host of spiritual darkness. Our armor is not the spiked helmet, the suit of mail, etc., but the helmet of salvation, the shield of faith, the breastplate of righteousness. Our feet are not "swift to shed blood," but are shod with the preparation of the Gospel of peace. I Thess. 5:8; Eph. 6:11, 17. Oh Christian, "put up thy sword into his [sic] place, for all they that take the sword shall perish with the sword." Matt. 26:52 [29]

McCafferty followed with the argument common among Pentecostals that the Christian's citizenship was not of this world but of heaven.

Again, in June 1915, the *Christian Evangel* reprinted material from Boddy's magazine, *Confidence*. Boddy was giving honorary assistance on the Continent to the Chaplain of the Expeditionary Forces. Boddy noted that: "He has been in constant touch with many of the soldiers, has found them responsive and open to the Gospel message. Letters from some converted soldiers at the front tell of how they give hymns in their 'dug-out' and go cheerfully into the danger zone."[30] The article also recounted the experiences of Andrew D. Urshan and G. R. Polman who were traveling in different war zones.

One question raised is if the earlier article reprinted from *Confidence* had engendered some degree of criticism besides that offered by Burt McCafferty, because immediately following this article is a note that this article should in no sense be interpreted to mean that Pentecostal saints are in favor of war. These articles were followed by the advertisement of the book by Booth-Clibborn, *Blood Against Blood*.[31]

Raymond T. Richey

Raymond Richey analyzed the military as a vast group of people who were ripe for gospel witness. He spent most of World War I working with soldiers. By 1917, Richey began to work in the military camps under the auspices of the Y.M.C.A. At the 1917 General Council of the Assemblies of God at St. Louis, Richey asked for support for his work. The resolution passed giving the blessing of the Assemblies of God to his work. Some were apparently troubled that he would work with the Y.M.C.A., for it was noted that this was the only available option. The resolution stated:

> Whereas President Wilson has urged the Y.M.C.A. to look after the spiritual welfare of all the soldiers; and whereas all we do in the camps must be done under the supervision of the Y.M.C.A.; therefore be it resolved that we adopt every available means consistent with Scriptural teaching and example to co-operate with every approved agency for revivals among the soldiers. To this end it is recommended that the saints everywhere determine, like the apostle Paul, to become all things to all men that by all means we may save some.[32]

There may have been resistance to working through the Y.M.C.A. because of the growing theological liberalism of the Y.M.C.A., as attested by an article condemning them for such in the *Pentecostal Evangel* in 1920.[33] There may have also been others who sensed that this would be a compromise with Pentecostal pacifism. The Y.M.C.A. during World War I became a conspicuously military organization. While the stated purpose was to look after the spiritual welfare of the soldiers, the Y.M.C.A. was not above other more mundane pursuits. Abrams cites the following instance:

> A Y.M.C.A. physical director, A. E. Marriott of Camp Sevier, supplied the soldiers with an "invaluable little manual" on Hand-to-Hand Fighting. The chief points of attack were minutely explained: "Eyes. Never miss an opportunity to destroy the eyes of the enemy. In all head holds use the finger on the eyes. They are the most delicate points in the body and easy to reach. The eye can easily be removed with the finger."[34]

Abrams also documented the work of the Y.M.C.A. in recruiting men for the military, as well as indoctrinating them to the Christian purpose of war.[35] The Y.M.C.A. was also known for harassment of conscientious objectors who were interned in the military camps. Meyer, who was a non-religious objector during World War I interned in Camp Sherman gives the following record:

> Two Y.M.C.A. officials had come to camp. The captain had ordered the war objectors to file into the mess hall for a lecture, and the Y.M.C.A. men had heaped reproaches on the Crusaders' heads for being too Christian and not going to war. The Crusaders, I was told, had accepted the lecture meekly enough, but Bill Davy had arisen and pulled the temple of oratory about their ears. There had been a violent argument, and many curious responses by the Y.M.C.A. gentleman, who tried to prove by quotation and logic that the Prince of Peace would have shouldered a musket and butchered the Hun to the tune of "The Yanks Are Coming!"[36]

While it is doubtful that Richie was given to those kinds of tactics, it is also doubtful that he was holding to any pacific sentiments. His main concern was to evangelize thousands of men who may have been going to their deaths in a short time.

It is clear that there were those in the movement who disagreed with the stand taken by the pacifists. According to Carl O'Guin, one of the leaders of this opposition was S. A. Jamieson.[37] Jamieson was a charter member of the General Council of the Assemblies of God and helped draw up the doctrinal statement.[38] As a former Presbyterian he was unaffected by Holiness tendencies toward pacifism.[39]

OTHERS

The Inexplicable Case of the Tomlinsons

The historical evidence for the Church of God (Cleveland, Tennessee) and the two church bodies which came out of it, the Church of God of Prophecy and the Church of God (Huntsville, Alabama), is most difficult to assess, as are its leaders, the Tomlinsons. The historical material for the Church of God is at notable points pacific, and yet is often atypical of the Pentecostal Movement in its nature, and as such deems separate treatment.

Ambrose Jessup Tomlinson (1865-1943)

In 1903, A. J. Tomlinson associated with the Holiness Church at Camp Creek, which had roots going back to 1886, but was established in 1902 under that name. In 1907, the name of the group was changed to Church of

God and the denomination was officially Pentecostal. In 1908, A. J. Tomlinson received the Pentecostal experience himself.[40] A. J. Tomlinson was reared a Quaker and remained such until uniting with the Holiness Church at Camp Creek in 1903.[41] Homer Tomlinson claimed his father graduated from a Quaker college, but according to Anderson this seems impossible.

> Homer A. Tomlinson, for example, called his father a college graduate, but the Quaker school he is said to have attended, Westfield Academy in Westfield, Indiana, did not even pretend to be a college at that time, and, furthermore, has no record of A. J. Tomlinson having been enrolled there. H. A. Tomlinson implied his father's name was deliberately removed from the records.[42]

It is impossible to say whether the Church of God (Cleveland) statement against members going to war originated with A. J. Tomlinson or from its Holiness origins. A. J. Tomlinson was the General Overseer of the denomination. It is interesting to note that the (Original) Church of God withdrew in 1909 from the Church of God (Cleveland) and carried a statement against Christians taking up arms and going to war. The (Original) Church of God withdrew the year previous to A. J. Tomlinson's assuming leadership.[43]

Apparently A. J. Tomlinson was accused of disloyalty during World War I in 1918. According to A. J. Tomlinson's diary, edited by his son Homer, A. J. Tomlinson was investigated by the Department of Justice. In A. J. Tomlinson's account: "About a month ago a government officer came in to make some investigations, and took a sample of everything we have, and some of our record books, that has caused us much inconvenience."[44] A. J. Tomlinson's defense indicates he was accused of disloyalty related to pacifism. This is plausible given the denomination's statement against members going to war. What is not clear is why A. J. Tomlinson would defend himself with accounts of his son's militarism if he was leader of a denomination which was pacifist. The diary offers the following information to disprove any disloyalty.

> (Homer was in the Tanks Corps, with Eisenhower in America, with Patton in France.) ....
> ... The investigation by government officers which came upon A. J. Tomlinson were instigated by bitter enemies, who used every means to discredit the work of the Church of God [sic]. A. J. Tomlinson's son, Homer, had been a cadet officer in the Cadet Corps at the University of Tennessee, was Summer School Secretary of the Culver Military Academy, and held this for three years, then became President of the Junior Plattsburg Military Training Camp, Plattsburg, N.Y., these two being the largest and most expensive private military summer schools in America. Both were very small, Homer's special task was to make them larger, and in such capacity gave much labor to the building up of the Boy Scouts movement in America. ... [45]

It is difficult to believe that Homer was aware that his father's church held a position against going to war when Homer wrote such a tribute to his personal military feats. Yet the defense also makes it clear that A. J. Tomlinson was being investigated for anti-war sentiments.

Yet Homer provided a stranger twist of events. In 1924, A. J. Tomlinson was dismissed from the leadership of the Church of God (Cleveland) because of financial indiscretion. He then founded the Church of God of Prophecy. With the death of A. J. Tomlinson, Homer disagreed with the choice of his brother, Milton, to be the leader of the Church of God of Prophecy. Homer formed the Church of God (Queens, N. Y.) which consisted of one congregation and it was later called the Church of God (Huntsville, Al.).[46]

In 1952, Homer took a trip around the world to proclaim peace to the world leaders.[47] He believed that the Millennium had arrived, and on July 4, 1964, he proclaimed that "all the kingdoms and dominions under the whole heavens do become the kingdoms of the saints of the Most High God."[48] He stated that 1939 to 1945 had been the great tribulation. He also noted that from 1952 to 1962 there had been no wars.[49] Homer proclaimed the union of church and state, and ran for President on the Theocratic Party.[50] Homer also denied the Deity of Christ.[51]

The Church of God (Huntsville, Al.) made bold statements for peace. The following are representative.

> One of the first steps in the kingdom of the saints would be the boldest, to change the world from a program of war to a program of peace. This would take the form of transposing the war budget of the United States, for example, to the building up of peoples in less fortunate circumstances both at home and abroad....
> We expect the people of God to do exploits for Peace on Earth as daring and risky as do men of war. Let our nation risk its neck for Peace like we call on our finest youth for war! Yes, that is my proposal, that with pure faith in God, we beat our swords into plowshares, and learn war no more.[52]

Significantly, in all this there is no teaching of the response of the Christian individual to refuse military service. This may have been because Homer believed there would be no more wars.[53] This is difficult to imagine, since the above statements were published in 1970, two years after Homer's death, and during the Vietnam War.

In summary, it is worth noting that Homer Tomlinson's position was in direct contrast to the early Pentecostals' position. The early Pentecostal leaders felt war was inevitable for this world, but proclaimed an individual ethic to be pursued by Christians. Homer, on the other hand, proclaimed an ethic of the end of war for the whole of society and neglected to direct the individual Christian against participation in war. Clearly, Homer Tomlinson was atypical for the Pentecostal Movement. Of significance, however, is the fact that even as unorthodox as Homer Tomlinson was, he bore witness to the currents of pacifism which surfaced in different ways in the Pentecostal Movement.

Footnotes

1. Robert Mapes Anderson, *Vision of the Disinherited*, p. 120; notes that Bell went to seminary at Southern Baptist Seminary in Louisville, Kentucky, and completed further schooling at the University of Chicago.
2. Menzies, *Anointed to Serve*, pp. 396, 89.
3. E. N. Bell, "Preachers Warned," *Weekly Evangel*, Jan. 5, 1918, p. 4.
4. *Ibid*.
5. *Ibid*.
6. *Ibid*.
7. E. N. Bell, "Questions and Answers," *Weekly Evangel*, Jan. 26, 1918, p. 9; see also Ray Abrams, *Preachers Present Arms*, p. 188, where he shows the tremendous pressure applied by local mob violence and bond salesmen to force pacifists to buy liberty bonds. Even Mennonites and Dunkards bought bonds due to the pressure.

8. E. N. Bell, "A Tremendous Day is To-Day," *Weekly Evangel*, Feb. 23, 1918, pp. 6-7.
9. E. N. Bell, "Loyalty Bonds," *Christian Evangel*, June 1, 1918, p. 8.
10. E. N. Bell, "Destroy This Tract," *Christian Evangel*, Aug. 24, 1918, p. 4.
11. E. N. Bell, "Questions and Answers," *Christian Evangel*, Oct. 19, 1918, p. 5.
12. Menzies, *Anointed to Serve*, pp. 396-397.
13. A number of leaders, including Williams, would miss the revival fervor of the early days, and try to rekindle them in the "Latter Rain Movement." The majority of the Assemblies of God leadership condemned this movement, with its many similarities to the early Pentecostal revival, as schismatic and even unbiblical.
14. E. S. Williams, "Our Duty as Christian Citizens," *Pentecostal Evangel*, Nov. 28, 1936, p. 1.
15. E. S. Williams, "The Conscientious Objector," *Pentecostal Evangel*, June 15, 1940, p. 4.
16. *Ibid.*, p. 5.
17. E. S. Williams, "Questions and Answers," *Pentecostal Evangel*, July 27, 1940, p. 5.
18. E. S. Williams, "Your Questions," *Pentecostal Evangel*, Feb. 12, 1961, p. 11.
19. *Ibid.*
20. Hollenweger, *Pentecostals*, p. 36.
21. Lycurgus Reuben Lynch, *Can a Christian Bear Arms?* (Springfield, Mo.: Artcraft Gospel Press, n.dd.), 8 pages, n.p.
22. *Ibid.*, n.p.
23. *Ibid.*
24. Hollengweger, *Pentecostals*, pp. 184-185.
25. *Ibid.*
26. "Is European War Justifiable?" *Christian Evangel*, Dec. 12, 1914, p. 1.
27. *Ibid.*, pp. 1, 3.
28. Assemblies of God General Council Minutes, 1914, p. 15; Brumback, pp. 196-197, notes McCafferty's spunk in arguing against the Pentecostal unitarians, caring little who opposed him.
29. Burt McCafferty, "Should Christians Go to War?" *Christian Evangel*, Jan. 16, 1915, p. 1.
30. "A. A. Boddy Goes to the Front," *Christian Evangel*, June 19, 1915, p. 1.
31. "Pentecostal Saints Opposed to War," *Christian Evangel*, June 19, 1915, p. 1.

32. Assemblies of God *General Council Minutes*, 1917, p. 16; also Raymond T. Richey, "Amongst the Soldier Boys," *Weekly Evangel*, Feb. 16, 1918, p. 16.

33. Max Wood Moorhead, "The Perils of Bolshevism at Home and Abroad," *Pentecostal Evangel*, Feb. 7, 1920, n.p.

34. Ray Abrams, *Preachers Present Arms*, p. 67.

35. *Ibid.*, p. 169 passim.

36. Ernest L. Meyer, *"Hey! Yellowbacks!"* (New York: John Day Co., 1930), pp. 106-107.

37. Phone conversation with Carl O'Guin, Jan. 16, 1982.

38. Assemblies of God *General Council Minutes*, 1914, p. 15; Minutes spell his name S. A. Jamison

39. Menzies, *Anointed to Serve*, p. 118; Brumback, *Suddenly From Heaven*, p. 204.

40. Charles W. Conn, *Like a Mighty Army*, p. 151; Conn's credibility as a historian is much greater than either of the Tomlinsons'.

41. Piepkorn, *Profiles in Belief*, vol. 3, pp. 178-179.

42. Anderson, *Vision*, p. 265, footnote no. 9; cites Homer A. Tomlinson to R. M. Anderson, Sept. 12, 1967.

43. Piepkorn, *Profiles in Belief*, pp. 181-182.

44. Tomlinson, *Diary*, p. 248.

45. *Ibid.*, pp. 248-249.

46. Piepkorn, *Profiles in Belief*, pp. 178-188.

47. *Church of God*, Oct. 15, 1963, p. 1.

48. *Church of God*, July 1, 1964, p. 1.

49. *Ibid.*, pp. 1-2.

50. *Church of God*, Oct. 15, 1963, pp. 1, 3, 4.

51. Piepkorn, *Profiles in Belief*, pp. 186, 192.

52. *The Book of Doctrines: 1903-1970* (Huntsville, Ala.: Church of God Publishing House, 1970), pp. 157-158.

53. How he interpreted Vietnam is a mystery.

CHAPTER V

THE EXPERIENCE OF PENTECOSTALS IN THE WORLD WARS

The statistical evidence for the practice of Pentecostals and pacifism is almost nonexistent for World War I, when pacifism was the strongest among their leaders. By World War II, the statistical evidence was more easily obtained, but there was little Pentecostal pacifism to record.

WORLD WAR I

The evidence for Pentecostal pacifism during World War I is difficult to assess. Most of the evidence is derived from non-Pentecostal sources with one notable exception, British Pentecostals. Since two of their national leaders were conscientious objectors during World War I, some attention was given to pacifism in their histories. There were also two cases of Pentecostals who gave evidence of their pacifism in their defense before authorities. Most evidence, however, was from secular or non-Pentecostal sources. In neither case was there a careful differentiation between Pentecostal and Holiness groups where their names were similar. For this reason, the evidence will appear incomplete and sketchy.

The Espionage and Sedition Acts

In a growing effort to bring all factious groups in the United States into line with the war effort, the Espionage Bill was passed on June 15, 1917. This law had the effect of denying free speech to those in opposition to the war. The law called for as much as $10,000 in fines and 20 years imprisonment for violation. A preacher vocal in his pacifism was easily implicated. The law called for prosecution of anyone who would "willfully cause or attempt to cause insubordination, disloyalty, mutiny, or refusal of duty in the military or naval forces... or shall wilfully obstruct the recruiting or enlistment services of the United States."[1] The following year, this law was amended in the Sedition Act. It was more repressive, but was justified because the country was at war. Anyone who opposed the war was seen as a German-collaborator or traitor.[2]

Clarence H. Waldron

Clarence Waldron, a Baptist-turned-Pentecostal, was tried for violation of the Espionage Act in January 1918. Three months earlier, Waldron's views came to public attention when he refused to have his church in Windsor, Vermont, participate in "Liberty Loan Sunday." At an evening service, a crowd gathered at his Baptist Church and forced him to drape in a flag and sing the "Star-Spangled Banner." Soon he was indicted "by a Federal grand jury... [and charged with] wilful and felonious interference with the military forces of the United States, by causing disloyalty among the young men who were members of his Bible class." Waldron's pacifism preceded his Pentecostal beliefs. In fact, ". . . Mr. Waldron was educated a non-resistant at Treveca College, Nashville, Tenn. (Church of the Nazarine). Mrs. Waldron came from a Mennonite home." The trial centered around advice given by Waldron to young men in his church and a tract which Waldron gave to them titled, *The Word of the Cross: Christ Again Before the Tribunal.* The young men testified against him, but their testimony conflicted. The case resulted in a verdict of not guilty with a jury vote of ten to two.[3] The government pressed for a retrial and he was found guilty and sentenced to ". . . fifteen years in the Georgia Penitentiary." Judge Howe noted, "The defendant, however honest he may be in his religion or pacifism, has actively engaged in opposing the nation in this great conflict." He went on to point out that "he may have been sincere in his beliefs but that makes him all the more effective and dangerous."[4]

William Reid

William Reid was pastor of a Pentecostal Mission in Sacramento, California, affiliated with the Pentecostal Assemblies of the World, a "oneness" group.[5] In December 1917, Reid was jailed following an investigation by local detectives.[6] What were the "seditious" remarks for which he was arrested? He had

> . . . expressed a hope that the United States and the Allies would win out in the gigantic struggle, but as far as he was

personally concerned he could not take up arms against an invading foe, owing to his religious tenets.[7]

Reid was also accused of giving advice to a parishioner who had been drafted, by reading from "article 13 of the Pentecostal Assemblage [sic] of the World."[8] The outcome of the Reid case is unknown.

Charles H. Mason

Bishop C. H. Mason, founder of the Church of God in Christ, the largest black Pentecostal group, gives evidence of having been called before the authorities for his pacifism during World War I. In 1918, he was jailed in Lexington, Mississippi, because "[he] took a scriptural stand against the ungodly deeds of the various races, about how many souls were being hurled into eternity without chance of seeking God for their soul's salvation." He preached "against trusting in the power of the United States, England, France or Germany, but trust in God."[9] Like some pacifists in World War I, he was accused of being a German sympathizer. It appears this motivated him to preach a sermon in Memphis later that year against the Kaiser.[10] The sermon reflected his pacifism in condemning the Kaiser for his militarism throughout in contrast to Christ the "Prince of Peace."[11]

Ambrose J. Tomlinson

The early leader of the Church of God (Cleveland) was also investigated by government officers. His defense, although inconsistent with pacifism, makes it apparent that the investigation was regarding pacifism.[12]

Brother Schaffer

A transient Pentecostal preacher, referred to as Brother Schaffer, was jailed in Davis City, Iowa, for something he said. He was visited in jail by some of the Pentecostal "brethren and convinced of his mistake; whereupon he was released and later displayed the American flag and asked the brethren to forgive him."[13] This story is consistent with those of Clarence Waldron and William Reid.

THE CONSCIENTIOUS OBJECTOR

England

The evidence of absolute pacifism among Pentecostals seems greater in England than in the United States. Donald Gee filed for conscientious objector status and was exempted to do farm labor. John and Howard Carter applied for exemption. John was totally exempted while Howard went to Wormwood Scrubbs Prison, London, and later Dartmoor Prison. Toward the end of the war, John did rehabilitation work with troubled teenagers in a farm colony.[14] A number of Pentecostal men were imprisoned in Wakefield Prison for being conscientious objectors. Among these were Ernest T. Mellor, Thomas Moggs, and Wilfred Richardson.[15]

United States

During World War I, the United States had no provision for absolute pacifism in the draft laws. There was provision for the religious objector who was a part of a religious group which prohibited members from participating in war in any form. But the law stated that ". . . no person so exempted shall be exempted from service in any capacity that the President shall declare to be noncombatant."[16] Given no choice, the Assemblies of God encouraged members to comply and go noncombatant.[17] There are no figures for the men who went noncombatant. The absolute pacifist who refused noncombatant service was still placed in the army camps as a form of coercion and many did not remain absolute pacifists. Only 20,873 men had been inducted who claimed noncombatant status (the only pacifist position recognized by the government).[18] "Just 3,989 of that number persisted in their position after reaching camp because of the extraordinary harshness with which objectors were treated."[19] Of these,

> 1300 'originally accepted or were assigned to noncombatant service'; 1200 were furloughed to agriculture and 99 to the Friends Reconstruction Unit in France, while 450 were sent to prison by courts-martial.[20]

Major Kellogg catalogued only 1,000 of all the conscientious objectors in the camps, as to religious affiliation. Of these, 13 are listed as Pentecostal, and another 20 are likely to have been Pentecostal based on their denominational name, while some of the 206 from less well-known sects may also have been Pentecostal.[21] Seventeen, of the 450 who were court-martialed as punishment for pacifism, were Pentecostals.[22]

Ernest Meyer, a non-religious pacifist, documented his experiences in the military camps and Fort Leavenworth, Kansas. He lists "Pentecostalites" and "holy rollers" among those with whom he spent time. Most notable was the Pentecostal, Pierson, "... who believe[d] in mysterious 'voices of the spirit.'"[23]

Carl O'Guin recalls Silas Biffle, who spent his time as a conscientious objector in Fort Riley, Kansas, and later became the pastor of the Assemblies of God in Joplin, Missouri.[24] A few Pentecostal men were "taken to military installations and stripped of all their clothing [except] their underwear and forced to go this way for days or else don the uniform which was laying [sic] close at hand."[25]

WORLD WAR II

Whereas during World War I conscientious objection in mainline denominations was almost nonexistent, in World War II members of mainline denominations were a greater part of those claiming conscientious objection. At the same time the Pentecostal leaders were not maintaining a concerted effort for pacifism. The position of the Assemblies of God among others by this time was at least in practice to counsel men to noncombatant service.[26] In all, 11,950 objectors (including non-theistic) served in Civilian Public Service Camps.[27] Of these, more than 131 were Pentecostals.[28] These men had to supply their own support and work without wages. In July 1943, Joseph Flower of the Assemblies of God put out a request for funds to help support the 20 from the denomination who were in the camps doing alternative service.[29] The total percentage of Pentecostals claiming conscientious objection in World War II was quite small compared to the same group in World War I.

Footnotes

1. H[orace] C. Peterson and Gilbert C. Fite, *Opponents of War: 1917-1918* (Madison: University of Wisconsin Press, 1957), p. 17.
2. *Ibid.*, pp. 215-221.
3. Harold L. Rotzel, "Vermont's Sedition Trial," *New York Evening Post*, 4 February 1918, p. 9.
4. "Pacifist Pastor Gets 15 Years," *Boston Globe*, 22 March 1918, pp. 1,5; "Testimony Given in Sedition Case," *Christian Science Monitor*, 10 January 1918, p. 6; Zechariah Chafee notes that Waldron "was pardoned after one year in Prison;" see, *Freedom of Speech* (New York: Harcourt, Brace & Co., n.d.), pp. 62, 393.
5. "Government to Investigate Reid," *Sacramento Bee*, 22 December 1917, pp. 1, 4.
6. "Sacramento Pastor Jailed on Charge of Sedition," *Sacramento Bee*, 21 December 1917.
7. *Sacramento Bee*, 22 December 1917, p. 4.
8. *Ibid.*
9. J[ames] O. Patterson, German R. Ross, and Julia Mason Atkins, *History and Formative Years of the Church of God in Christ: With Excerpts from the Life and Works of Its Founder--Bishop C. H. Mason* (Memphis: Church of God in Christ Publishing House, 1969), pp. 23-24. For further accounts of trouble over pacifism with authorities, see p. 24.
10. *Ibid.*, p. 28; Mason said, "I cannot understand, after preaching the gospel for twenty years and exhorting men to peace and righteousness, how I could be accused of fellowshipping the anti-Christ of the Kaiser."
11. *Ibid.*, pp. 26-28.
12. Homer Tomlinson, *Diary of A. J. Tomlinson*, vol. 2 (Queens, N. Y.: Church of God World Headquarters, 1949), pp. 248-250.
13. Eugene N. Hastie, *History of the West Central District Council of the Assemblies of God* (n.p., 1948), pp. 95-96.
14. John Carter, *Howard Carter: Man of the Spirit* (Nottingham: Assemblies of God Publishing House, n.d.), pp. 39-49.
15. Donald Gee, *Wind and Flame*, pp. 39-49.
16. Lillian Schlissel, *Conscience in America* (New York: E. P. Dutton & Co., 1968), pp. 162-163.
17. "Compulsory Military Service: An English Conscientious Objector's Testimony," *Weekly Evangel*, April 28, 1917, p. 7. What the article failed to recognize was that contrary to English experience,

the noncombatant in the United States was not always easily distinguished from other soldiers in assignment.

18. Staughton Lynd, *Nonviolence in America: A Documentary History* (Indianapolis: Bobbs-Merrill Co., Inc., n.d.), p. xxxiv.

19. *Ibid.*

20. Norman M. Thomas, *Is Conscience a Crime?*, new ed., enl., with a forward by Charles Chatfield (New York: Garland Publishing, Inc., 1972), p. 15.

21. Paul C. French, *We Won't Murder* (New York: Hastings House, 1940), pp. 85-87. Of the list, 20 are members of the "Negro Church of God," which this author suspects to be the Church of God in Christ. For an old source listing black holiness churches with names similar, see J. L. Neve, *Churches and Sects of Christendom* (Blair, Neb.: Lutheran Pub. House, 1952), pp. 368-369.

22. Thomas, *Is Conscience a Crime?*, pp. 48; gives a chart prepared by Prof. Jacob G. Ewert, of Tabor College, Hillsboro, Kansas. In this, 13 are Pentecostal, and four Apostolic Faith. If the numbers seem insignificant, compare this with the 13 listed for the Quakers (Friends). This, however, is likely because the Quakers had a reconstruction unit in France to which the Government sent 99 men. Also: Ray H. Abrams, Preachers Present Arms, rev. 2nd ed. (Scottdale, Pa.: Herald Press, 1969), p. 135.

23. Ernest L. Meyer, *"Hey! Yellowbacks!"* (New York: John Day Co., 1930), pp. 83, 86, 108, 136, 162.

24. Carl O'Guin, phone interview, January 16, 1982.

25. John Irvine Harrison, "A History of the Assemblies of God" (unpublished Th.D. dissertation, Berkley Divinity School, 1954), p. 151.

26. Selective Service System, *Conscientious Objection*, Special Monograph no. 11 (Washington: Government Printing Office, 1950), p. 324f. This quotes Joseph Flower of the Assemblies of God, "The Universal advice given to our young men was that instead of taking the extreme conscientious objector position that it was better for them to ask for noncombatant service."

27. Schlissel, *Conscience in America*, p. 215.

28. Selective Service System, *Conscientious Objection*, pp. 318-320; lists by denomination, the following: Apostolic Faith 10, Assemblies of God 21, Church of God of the Apostolic Faith 1, Church of the Foursquare Gospel 1, Community Full Gospel Church 1, Faith Tabernacle 16, First Ukranian Evangelical Pentecostal 1, Foursquare Church 1, Foursquare Gospel 1, Full Gospel Church 4, Holy Rollers 1, Open Bible Standard 1, Pentecostal 67, Pentecostal Assemblies of God 2, Philadelphia Church 1, Church in Jesus Name

1, Christian Assembly 1. This is not including some from the 154 lumped together as Church of God, most of whom I suspect were the Pentecostal variety. This would bring the total to more than 250. Another list, taken from those who registered C. O., included numerous other Pentecostal groups, but without listing figures; see pp. 24-27. The value of this list is limited because it lists 354 denominations total, which is nearly comprehensive for all denominations. Menzies notes that in the Assemblies of God 35 served in these camps, p. 328, citing "Quarterly Letter," March 24, 1951.

29. J. Roswell Flower, "The Plight of the Conscientious Objector: In the Present World Conflict," *Pentecostal Evangel*, July 3, 1943, pp. 2-3.

CHAPTER VI

THE LOSS OF PENTECOSTAL PACIFISM

The Change in Social Status

The time since the World Wars was marked by great strides in upward mobility for the Pentecostals, which may have been the greatest factor in the change that took place in Pentecostal thinking about pacifism. Religiously and socially, Pentecostals were moving into the mainstream and it seems likely that their values would reflect that move.[1] While it is beyond the scope of this study to deal with this mobility, none of the personalities or related issues escaped the influence of this sociological factor.

Both World Wars contributed to the rise in social status of Pentecostal clergy. Donald Gee notes that the government (in England) gave exemption to ministers during World War I.

> This circumstance, however, invested the status of a recognized minister within the Pentecostal Movement with an entirely new significance. Until the war, especially in the Assemblies of God, recognition as a minister was held very loosely.[2]

It is significant that the original framing of the Assemblies of God statement on pacifism in the United States was written at the entrance to World War I. Many ministers were credentialed at that time, and were as relieved at the ministerial exemptio as they were at their recognition as a pacifist denomination.[3] It is possible that military exemptions motivated a number to be credentialed at this time just as rail discounts had at other times.[4]

The governmental response to Pentecostals in the World Wars not only raised the social status of Pentecostal ministers but made two separate moral communities: the clergy and the laity. Bryan R. Wilson, in speaking of World War II in England, noted the dynamics taking place.

> The war brought new strains--the professionalized ministry proved unable to win the movement to pacifism--the laity were more fully prepared to compromise with the wider society. The ministry repeatedly showed itself disposed to the extremism of the sect--in pacifism, divine healing, and social practices generally--but always conceded much to the folk ways from which the laity could not readily be weaned... The war professionalized the ministry yet further, and widened the gap between them and the laity, by the recognition granted to the ministry in exemption from war services. The laity were deprived of any practical example in the matter of conscientious objection--there was thus institutional support for a different ethic for ministry and laity.[5]

Whereas in World War I numerous Pentecostal young men who had not yet been pastors were to practice conscientious objection at some cost to themselves, by World War II, this practice was reserved for the clergy at little cost. Thus this (English) Pentecostal group clearly stated its belief in "the incompatibility of the Gospel call and the Christian's participation in war," yet left the matter for each individual to settle "... for himself in the light of the Word of God."[6] In this way, pacifism could be relegated to a professional clergy who obviously lived a more separated calling anyway. There was already a precedent in most other churches for such a distinction recognized by the governmental exemption for ministers.

World War II

By World War II, three related factors converged to cause irreparable damage to the movement's witness to pacifism. These factors were the large number of Pentecostals in active duty in the War, the institution of the chaplaincy, and the identification with the National Association of Evangelicals. Pentecostals were moving from the periphery of both church and state to the mainstream.

Active Duty in World War II

Although acknowledging the fact that no one knows how many men registered noncombatant in World War II, it is difficult to imagine that anyone was preaching pacifism from Pentecostal pulpits given the wholesale enlistment of Pentecostal men. During this time a magazine, *Reveille*, published especially for servicemen, was inaugurated by the Assemblies of God. By asking pastors for the names of Assemblies of God men in the service, the Servicemen's Department compiled a directory of 76,000 men. Over 1,000 of them had been killed in the war by this time.[7] A survey showed that a large number of the servicemen intended to go into the ministry upon discharge. Central Bible Institute was making plans for expansion to meet this need, anticipating the G. I. Bill.[8] Harrison notes with approbation the change from World War I, that

> ... the blood of the noble youth from the ranks of the Assemblies of God flowed with that of all others ... and they wrote a like glorious page in the history of our land with those of the other great churches of America.[9]

In the Church of God (Cleveland), the servicemen worked closely with missionaries and were sometimes responsible for beginning new mission works.[10]

The Pentecostal Holiness Church gave legitimacy to the struggle in their statement of 1937 which opposed, "... Communism, Fascism and Naziism as now predominant in Russia, Italy and Germany."[11] Paul described them as "... far from being pacifist, much less disloyal."[12] They favored isolation at the beginning of the War, warning against "... succumbing to 'allied propaganda' and 'pulling the chestnuts' of England and France out of the fire.... Yet when war came, the church gave total support to the war effort," and "... thousands of young men to fight in the armed forces."[13]

Chaplaincy

The first military chaplain from the Assemblies of God, Clarence P. Smales, was commissioned in 1941.[14] By 1944 the Assemblies of God had 34 chaplains.[15] The Pentecostal Holiness Church supplied at least 12 chaplains during World War II.[16] Menzies argues that with the first Pentecostal chaplains there is admission of a change from pacifism to non-pacifism.[17] It is doubtful that there could have been Mennonite or Quaker military chaplains. The existence of the chaplaincy suggested at least tacit approval of the military.[18] Others have argued that chaplains were the chief resource for the military to provide the kind of "public relations" they needed with churches.[19] It would only be a matter of time before they would write a biblical justification of the work of a soldier.

National Association of Evangelicals

Despite the protests of right-winged Carl McIntire, who rigorously opposed membership of the Assemblies of God in the National Association of Evangelicals,[20] membership was granted in 1942.[21] Menzies interprets this event in the light of the denomination's participation in World War II.

> What were the reasons that evangelicals extended the invitation to the Pentecostals to share in the development of the NAE? There are several contributing factors. One was the role of the Assemblies of God in World War II. Assemblies of God men were thrown together with others in the military services, creating a mutual feeling of respect between Evangelicals and Pentecostals. Without question, the contact of Pentecostals with the larger church world occasioned by the grim circumstances of the war broke down many barriers on both sides. Another avenue of openness occasioned by the conflict was the service of Assemblies of God ministers for the first time in the army chaplaincy corps, a venture the pacifist-oriented denomination had not engaged in here to fore.[22]

Menzies also notes the positive effect of the Assemblies of God making available the magazine, *Reveille*, to any servicemen regardless of denomination, which cost the Assemblies of God $450,000 during the war.[23]

Augustus Cerillo links the loss of pacifism with the loss of other Pentecostal distinctives. He states,

> Indeed, we might see parallels between this personal cultural conformity and the denomination's quest for national acceptance. Two examples hopefully will suffice. Has not our earlier and socially unpopular pacifism been replaced by a rather uncritical support of the nation's military and foreign policies? And a not unreasonable intuitive leap allows me to believe that we mute our pentecostal zeal just sufficiently to guarantee increasing acceptance by the National Association of Evangelicals.[24]

It is significant that in the same year the Assemblies of God joined the National Association of Evangelicals, the Assemblies of God also reviewed the adequacy of their statement on military service.[25]

In England in 1940, James McWhirter published *The Bible and War*, arguing against pacifism. He was a Pentecostal in the leadership of the Elim Foursquare Gospel Church with which John and Howard Carter earlier related.[26]

Assemblies of God Since World War II

Again in 1947 there was a report on an attempt to reformulate the statement on military service in the Assemblies of God. The committee, chaired by Atwood Foster, felt "...unable to formulate an article on Military Service that will better represent the attitude of the Assemblies of God than that which is now a part of our General Council By-Laws."[27] Although it is impossible to tell how widespread the resistance was, there is evidence of resistance to changing this article. During World War II, Leslie C. Wattenburger corresponded with the editor of the *Pentecostal Evangel*, concerning his misgivings about the treatment of the issue of conscientious objection in the *Pentecostal Evangel*. Wattenburger claimed he was a conscientious objector and that he was willing to die for his convictions.[28] Stanley Frodsham, one of the early framers of the pacifist statement of the Assemblies of God, gave an answer which is revealing. At the time of World War I, Frodsham was an absolute pacifist. Now, although feeling it important for the "boys" to register noncombatant, Frodsham argued that he did not believe that one who took part in a war of defense would be judged as a murderer. According to Frodsham,

> ... It is quite a different thing to be full of hatred against someone and deliberately destroy that one in time of peace, and for a man to conscientiously defend his home, his wife and his children in time of war; and I believe the reading of the Scriptures makes this distinction quite clear.[29]

Frodsham did not make clear which Scripture he was referring to in the letter to Wattenburger.

If the official pacifism could not be changed at this time, other resolutions could be passed which would temper its effect. In 1945, a resolution was passed titled "Religious Liberty." This resolution petitioned the President of the United States to continue occupation of Italy at the request of Assemblies of God chaplains and military personnel, in order to ensure religious liberty for Protestants. The last lines of the resolution reflected the degree of Pentecostal involvement in the war. The resolution stated that it was "...for this cause and in this behalf, sacrifices having been made by the pledging of our lives, our fortunes, our sons and our sacred honor." Contrary to earlier Pentecostals who looked for the immediate return of Christ and viewed national existence as tentative, Pentecostals now sought the preservation of

". . . a government of, for, and by a free people which shall not perish from the earth."[30]

From 1951 to 1959, the Chaplaincy Commission of the National Association of Evangelicals represented the Assemblies of God in Washington, D.C., until the Assemblies of God established their own Chaplaincy Commission.[31]

In 1953, the Assemblies of God statement on Military Service was altered without comment. Reference to the Decalogue (Ex.20:13) as a reason for not participating in bloodshed during time of war was removed.[32] This probably reflected both a greater theological precision than that of the earlier Pentecostals, as well as a growing belief that killing in war was not murder. Both E. N. Bell and E. S. Williams had argued that killing in war, under orders, was not murder.

In 1957, when the Assemblies of God in the United States was extolling the benefits of civil defense shelters, the British Assemblies of God was calling for a ban on the H-Bomb. In the United States a resolution passed, backing participation in such shelters because "in the event of a nuclear attack upon our country spiritual leaders and workers will be in great demand to comfort the wounded, dying, distressed. . . ."[33] The British rejected an appeal for civil defense workers. In reference to a pamphlet titled, "The Plain Man's Guide to the H-Bomb," they said, "Our greater need is not a guide to the H-Bomb, but a guide from it." The British article called for love of enemies and overcoming evil with good. The verdict was "to ban all bombs. . . . Assemblies of God are officially a Pacifist movement (though not a movement of pacifists)."[34] Richard Champion, staff member at the *Pentecostal Evangel* in the United States, read the British Pentecostal editorial and noted that "this is an 'ostrich' editorial if I ever read one."[35] To the American Pentecostals, the arguments of their earlier counterparts now seemed foolish.

In 1961, Ralph Colburn submitted an article to the *Pentecostal Evangel* on conscientious objection, titled "You and Your Military Service." The article was blocked from publication by the Executive Presbytery whose "... unanimous opinion was that it would not be desirable to air this issue in the *Pentecostal Evangel*."[36] At the 1965 General Council, a resolution passed in which the Executive Presbytery appointed a committee to study the statement on Military Service.[37] The next year the National Association of Evangelicals, in response to the growing national discontent with Vietnam, issued a statement recognizing the "right of dissent" but not the "'privilege' of civil disobedience."[38] The *Pentecostal Evangel* carried the release. During this time Warren F. McPherson, Secretary of Public Relations for the Assemblies of God, wrote an article titled "Military Service Policy Restudied by Assemblies." The article explained the current view of the Assemblies of God relative to war. It also featured a conference taking place in Springfield, Missouri, led by Rev. Robert R. Way, the denomination's servicemen's representative. One of the offerings was a class on "Preparing Youth for Military Service." According to Rev. Way, "...the church must influence the attitude of its young men toward all of life's processes. Cooperation with properly established authority is right and scriptural." He could see no difference in"....preparing for a tour of duty in the armed forces than in getting ready for any other phase of life."

This was during the Vietnam Era. McPherson finally noted that

> the Assemblies of God is in a continuing program encouraging its members to recognize military service as an opportunity for worldwide missionary service rather than "a lost chapter in the prime years of a young man's life."[39]

In 1966, the issue of war and the sixth commandment was dealt with in the *Holiness Handbook*, published by the Assemblies of God. An adapted version appeared later in *At Ease* magazine in an article titled "The Sixth Commandment," which justifies military killing for the Christian. In complete reversal it was argued,

> We are told to protect the weak. Can we do it without opposing the strong? Is it possible that an extension of the sixth commandment suggests that he who neglects to save life is the same as he who takes it away?[40]

Contrary to the earlier interpretation of Scripture, it was argued that Christ recognized war as a necessary means of wresting power from evil men.

> He said, "If my kingdom were of this world, then would my servants fight" (John 18:36). He is not saying here that fighting is wrong, but that it was the wrong time for that fighting. The time will come when Jesus Christ will engage in war (Revelation 19:15).[41]

Although the article intended to show that the military killer was not included in the sixth commandment, it implied that those committing suicide, dying from lung cancer (apparently from cigarettes) or the "operator of a speeding car" were all included in the injunction.[42]

By now it seemed inevitable that the Assemblies of God would change from its historic belief in pacifism. In 1967 it officially did. The new statement retained the element of loyalty to government while dropping any pacific sentiments. It read as follows:

> As a movement we affirm our loyalty to the government of the United States in war or peace. We shall continue to insist, as we have historically, on the right of each member to choose for himself whether to declare his position as a combatant, a noncombatant, or a conscientious objector.[43]

This differed radically from the original statement since it did not condemn killing in war, and it cited no Scriptures. Murray Dempster lamented the new way of framing ethical arguments. He noted that,

> apparently, the pentecostal believer's conscience on war no longer needed to be formed specifically by biblical teaching but was to be informed by knowledge of certain political, theological and ethical propositions.[44]

The question now remained, whether the denomination would support those who became conscientious objectors. In 1972, William Suttles was imprisoned, apparently for refusing alternative service as a conscientious objector. He wrote to the editor of the *Pentecostal Evangel*, and the response was one of trying to persuade him (however gently) to comply with the government's wishes.[45]

In 1977, Dave Ytterock surveyed a large Assemblies of God Sunday school class on ethical attitudes. Some of the answers were revealing in areas related to pacifism. He found that 73 percent would use a gun to protect their family, and 60 percent would use a gun to protect a neighbor, while 95 percent believed "a Christian generally may fight in defense of his country."[46] At the General Council of the Assemblies of God in 1981, a resolution was introduced in support for the bill to establish the World Peace Tax Fund. The basis for the resolution was that there were still those in the denomination who were conscientiously opposed to war on the basis of Scripture.[47] The resolution was defeated, even though it stopped short of calling for civil disobedience.

Ironically, in a time when many Evangelicals are questioning the validity of warfare as a Christian enterprise, most Pentecostals are forgetting their heritage of pacifism.[48]

Footnotes

1. Robert M. Anderson, *Vision of the Disinherited* (New York: Oxford University Press, 1979), pp. 195-222. The whole work is a study of the Pentecostal Movement from a sociological perspective. Gary Schwartz, *Sect Ideologies and Social Status* (Chicago: University of Chicago Press, 1970), pp. 74, 137-181; H. Richard Niebuhr, *The Social Sources of Denominationalism* (Hamden, Conn.: Yale University, 1929; reprint ed., Ann Arbor: Cushing-Malloy, Inc., 1954), pp. 26-76, 106-134; Bryan R. Wilson, *Sects and Society: A Sociological Study of Three Religious Groups in Britain* (Westport, Conn.: Greenwood Press, 1961), pp. 77-118; Menzies, *Anointed to Serve*, pp. 344-373; Hollenweger, The Pentecostals, pp. 26, 59; Werner Stark, *The Sociology of Religion* (New York: Fordham University Press, 1967), pp. 198-214.
2. Gee, *Wind and Flame*, p. 193.
3. *Weekly Evangel*, Aug. 4, 1917, p. 6.
4. *Weekly Evangel*, May 19, 1917, p. 8; invites any congregations that wish such recognition to join the Assemblies of God, but not simply to avoid war if they do not wish to share the responsibilities of relating to the group.
5. Wilson, *Sects and Society*, p. 330.
6. *Ibid.*, p. 88, citing *Elim Evangel* XXX, 1949, p. 513.

The Loss Of Pentecostal Pacifism 119

7. Assemblies of God *General Council Minutes*, 1945, p. 81. Menzies notes 50,000 men in the service in 1944, Anointed to Serve, p. 327; citing, *Pentecostal Evangel*, Mar. 18, 1944, p. 12.

8. *Ibid.*, pp. 82-87.

9. John I. Harrison, "A History of the Assemblies of God" (Th.D. dissertation, Berkley Baptist Divinity School, 1954), pp. 156f.

10. Conn, *Like a Mighty Army*, pp. 337-348.

11. George H. Paul, "The Religious Frontier in Oklahoma: Dan T. Muse and the Pentecostal Holiness Church" (Ph.D. dissertation, University of Oklahoma, 1965), p. 143.

12. *Ibid.*, p. 142.

13. Vinson Synan, *The Old-Time Power* (Franklin Springs, Ga.: Advocate Press, 1973), p. 206; citing, *The Advocate*, Jan. 1, 1942, p. 1.

14. Menzies, *Anointed to Serve*, p. 327; citing, *Pentecostal Evangel*, October 17, 1942, p. 3; also, Leon G. Kircher, Jr., "The History of the Organizational Development and Ministry to the Military by the Assemblies of God: December 1941-December 1979" (Research Paper, Assemblies of God Graduate School, 1979), p. 10.

15. Assemblies of God *General Council Minutes*, 1945, p. 83.

16. Joseph E. Campbell, *The Pentecostal Holiness Church 1898-1948* (Franklin Springs, Ga.: Pentecostal Holiness Church Publishing House, 1951), p. 408; Mr. Ellenberg trained but was unable to perform as chaplain because of convictions.

17. Menzies, *Anointed to Serve*, p. 327

18. Menzies, phone interview, November 1980.

19. John M. Swomley, Jr., *The Military Establishment* (Boston: Beacon Press, 1964), pp. 200-209.

20. Menzies, *Anointed to Serve*, p. 184.

21. *Ibid.*, p. 185; The Assemblies of God passed a resolution to join in 1943; Assemblies of God *General Council Minutes*, 1943, p. 8.

22. Menzies, *Anointed to Serve*, p. 188.

23. *Ibid.*

24. Agustus Cerillo, Jr., "Moving Up: Some Consequences of the New A/G Social Status," *Agora*, Winter 1978, p. 11.

25. Menzies, *Anointed to Serve*, p. 327; citing, *General Presbytery Minutes*, 1943, p. 10; see, *General Council Minutes*, 1943, p. 8; however, p. 26 is a case of a resolution against compulsory military training of youth, which was being considered in Congress.

26. Wilson, *Sects and Society*, pp. 55, 89; citing, James McWhirter, *The Bible and War*, 1940. I have not been able to find this book. Wilson notes that McWhirter's belief in British Israelism probably led to a

patriotism and rejection of pacifism. McWhirter was a close associate of Jeffreys in the Elim Foursquare Church in England.

27. Assemblies of God *General Council Minutes*, 1947, p. 13.

28. Leslie C. Wattenburger to Editor of the *Pentecostal Evangel* [Stanley H. Frodsham], 24 November 1941, files of the *Pentecostal Evangel*.

29. Stanley H. Frodsham to Mr. Leslie C. Wattenburger, 26 November 1941, files of the *Pentecostal Evangel*.

30. Assemblies of God *General Council Minutes*, 1945, p. 39

31. Assemblies of God *General Council Minutes*, 1951, p. 33f; General Council Minutes, 1959, pp. 28-30.

32. Assemblies of God *General Council Minutes*, 1953, p. 80.

33. Assemblies of God *General Council Minutes*, 1957, p. 55f.

34. *Redemption Tidings*, November 15, 1957, pp. 2-3; Donald Gee and Howard Carter were members of the Executive Council in Britain which published this editorial.

35. Note on stationary of Richard G. Champion attached to the above editorial; in the files of the *Pentecostal Evangel*.

36. Memorandum, Bert Webb to Bob Cunningham, May 31, 1961; Memorandum, Bert Webb to Bob Cunningham, July 17, 1961; from the files of the *Pentecostal Evangel*.

37. Assemblies of God *General Council Minutes*, 1965, p. 61.

38. *Church News Service* (Public Information Service of the National Association of Evangelicals), Feb. 1, 1966. Also noted were Evangelicals whose historic position was against participation in war, while commending those who disassociated themselves from disloyalty or civil disobedience.

39. Warren F. McPherson, "Military Service Policy Restudied by Assemblies," n.d. (internal evidence dates it after 1965 and before August 1967), n.p., from the files of the *Pentecostal Evangel*. Significantly this was going on just previous to the official change in the denomination's position on pacifism. It seems the decision had been made before ever being voted on by the General Council.

40. *At Ease*, Summer, n.d., p. 9; article adapted from Holiness Handbook (Springfield, Mo.: Gospel Publishing House, 1966).

41. *Ibid.*, p. 10.

42. *Ibid.*, p. 11.

43. Assemblies of God *General Council Minutes*, 1967, pp. 14-15, 33; The revision committee included Howard Bush (chairman), O. B. Harrup, Daniel P. Kolenda, Howard Cummings, Bartlett Peterson, J. L. Gerhart, William H. Robertson, and Chaplain Leonard L. Ahrmbrsc (text unclear); "New Bylaws on Military Service Adopted by General Council," *Pentecostal Evangel*, Oct. 8, 1967.

44. Murray W. Dempster, "Peacetime Draft Registration and Pentecostal Moral Conscience," *Agora*, Spring 1980, pp. 2-3; Dempster is not arguing for pacifism, but biblical foundations.
45. Robert Cunningham to William Suttles, Sept. 8, 1972.
46. Dave Ytterock, "Probing Our Moral Identity," *Agora*, Fall 1977, p. 7; there were 260 persons surveyed.
47. *Resolutions Processed for Presentation to the 39th General Council*, 1981, pp. 35-36; sponsored by Michael H. Chase and Joe A. Krueggel.
48. Hollenweger, *Pentecostals*, p. 37; makes a similar point. He contrasts Assemblies of God patriotism in the United States with the growing pacifism of German and Swedish Pentecostals.

CONCLUSION

The loss of pacifism by the Pentecostals, like its origin, may be related to its roots in the Holiness Movement. First, the Holiness Movement did not maintain strong pacifism after World War I. The same sociological factors which caused changes in the Holiness Movement effected the Pentecostals. Second, the ties between the two groups were quickly cut due to the renunciation of "tongues" by the Holiness Movement. Feeling distanced from their closest relatives, the Pentecostals sought new identifications. It is possible that these new associations, especially with other evangelicals, also influenced their world view. But Pentecostals need to ponder whether they can long maintain their distinctive views about the church and the Holy Spirit, while conforming to mainstream Evangelical socio-religious views. By asking in what ways their earlier pacifism formed a part of their whole belief system, Pentecostals may come to see that this loss signaled other losses too. It may be time to ask in what way this movement, founded upon a desire to be open to the renewing ministry of the Holy Spirit, can continue to have a prophetic role in the life of the church.

BIBLIOGRAPHY

Books

Abrams, Ray H. *Preachers Present Arms*. Rev. and enl. Scottdale, Pa.: Herald Press, 1969.

Allen Devere. *The Fight for Peace*. Vol. II, The Garland Library of War and Peace. New intro. by Charles Chatfield. New York: Garland Publishing Co., 1971.

Anderson, Robert Mapes. *Vision of the Disinherited*. New York: Oxford University Press, 1979.

The Apostolic Church: Its Principles and Practices. Bradfore, Great Britain: Apostolic Publications, 1961.

Bartleman, Frank. *Two Years Mission Work in Europe Just Before the World War 1912-14*. Los Angeles: By the Author, n.d.

The Book of Doctrines 1903-1970: Issued in the Interest of the Church of God. Huntsville, Ala: Church of God Publishing House, 1970.

Booth-Clibborn, Arthur Sydney. *Blood Against Blood*. New York: Charles C. Cook, n.d. Available from Asbury Theological Seminary library, Wilmore, Ky., Southern California College library, Costa Mesa, Ca., North American Baptist Seminary library, Sioux Falls, SD.

Brock, Peter. *Pacifism in Europe in 1914*. Princeton: Princeton University Press, 1972.

_____. *Pacifism in the United States from the Colonial Era to the First World War*. Princeton: Princeton University Press, 1968.

Brumback, Carl. *Suddenly From Heaven*: A History of the Assemblies of God. Springfield, Mo.: Gospel Publishing House, 1961.

Campbell, Joseph E. *The Pentecostal Holiness Church 1898-1948: Its Background and History*. Franklin Springs, Ga.: Publishing House of the Pentecostal Holiness Church, 1951.

Carter, John. *Donald Gee: Pentecostal Statesman*. Nottingham, England: Assemblies of God Publishing House, 1975.

_____. *Howard Carter: Man of the Spirit*. Nottingham, England: Assemblies of God Publishing House, n.d.

Chafee, Zechariah. *Freedom of Speech*. New York: Harcourt, Brace and Company, n.d.

Chesham, Sallie. *Born to Battle*. Chicago: Rand McNally and Co., 1965.

Clanton, Arthur L. *United We Stand: A History of Oneness Organizations*. Hazlewood, Mo.: Pentecostal Publishing House, 1970.

Coad, R. Roy. *A History of the Brethren Movement: Its Origins, its Worldwide Development and its Significance for the Present Day*. Exeter, England: Paternoster Press Ltd., 1968.

Collier, Richard. *The General Next to God*. New York: E. P. Dutton, 1965.

Conn, Charles W. *Like a Mighty Army: A History of the Church of God*. Rev. ed. Cleveland, Tenn.: Pathway Press, 1977.

Cook, Philip Lee. "Zion City, Illinois: Twentieth Century Utopia." Ph.D. Thesis, University of Colorado, 1965.

Cornell, Julien. *The Conscientious Objector and the Law*. Reprint ed. The Peace Movement in America Series, Forward by Hary Emerson Fosdick. New York: Jerome S. Ozer, 1972.

Curti, Merle Eugene. *The American Peace Crusade 1815-1860*. New York: Octagon Books, Inc., 1965.

_____. *Peace or War: The American Struggle 1636-1936*. The Garland Library of War and Peace. New intro. by Merle Eugene Curti. New York: Garland Publishing, Inc., 1972.

DeGrott, A[lfred] T. *Disciple Thought: A History*. Forth Worth: By the Author, 1965.

Dictionary of American Communal and Utopian History, 1980 ed. s.v. "John Alexander Dowie."

Dieter, Melvin Easterday. *The Holiness Revival of the Nineteenth-Century*. Studies in Evangelicalism, vol. 1, Metuchen, N.J.: Scarecrow Press, 1980.

Dresser, Amos. *The Bible Against War*. Oberlin: By the Author, 1849.

Encyclopedia of American Religions. 1978 ed. s.v. "Missionary Church."

Ewart, Frank J. *The Phenomenon of Pentecost*: (A History of "The Latter Rain"). St. Louis: Pentecostal Publishing House, 1947.

Ford, Jack. *In the Steps of John Wesley: The Church of the Nazarene in Britain*. Kansas City, Mo.: Nazarene Publishing House, 1968.

Garrison, Winfred Ernest and DeGrott, Alfred T. Rev. *The Disciples of Christ: A History*. St. Louis: Bethany Press, 1964.

Gause, R. H. *Church of God Polity*. Cleveland, Tenn.: Pathway Press, 1973.

Bibliography

Harper, Michael. *As At the Beginning.* London: Hodder and Stoughton, 1956.

Harrison, John Irvine. "A History of the Assemblies of God." Th.D. dissertation, Berkley Baptist Divinity School, 1954.

Hartzler, J. S. *Mennonites in the World War: or Nonresistnce Under Test.* Scottdale, Pa.: Mennonite Publishing House, 1921.

Hastie, Eugene N. *History of the West Central District Council of the Assemblies of God.* n.p., 1948.

Hollenweger, Walter J. "Handbuch der Pfingstbewegung." Ph.D dissertation, University of Zurich, 1965. (Photocopy)

_____. *The Pentecostals: The Charismatic Movement in the Churches.* Minneapolis: Augsburg, 1972.

Kendrick, Klaude. *The Promise Fulfilled: A History of the Modern Pentecostal Movement.* Springfield, Mo.: Gospel Publishing House, 1961.

Kircher, Leon G. "The History of the Organizational Development and Ministry to the Military by the Assemblies of God December 1941- December 1979." Springfield, Mo., 1979. (Typewritten)

Lane, Christel. *Christian Religion in the Soviet Union: A Sociological Study.* London: George Allen Unwin, 1978.

Lang, G[eorge] H[enry]. *An Ordered Life.* London: Paternoster Press, 1959.

Lynd, Staughton, ed. *Nonviolence in America: A Documentary History.* The American Heritage Series. Indianapolis: Bobbs-Merrill Company, Inc., 1966.

Manual: United Pentecostal Church International. Hazlewood, Mo.: Pentecostal Publishing House, 1972.

Marchand, C. Roland. *The American Peace Movement and Social Reform 1898-1918.* Princeton: Princeton University Press, 1973.

Marechale, The [Catherine Booth-Clibborn]. *They Endured.* London: Marshall, Morgan Scott, Lts., n.d.

Mead, Frank S. *Handbook of Denominations in the United States*, 5th ed. Nashville: Abingdon Press, 1970.

Mennonite Encyclopedia. 1956 ed. s.v. "Holiness Movement."

Menzies, William. *Anointed to Serve: The Story of the Assemblies of God.* Springfield, Mo.: Gospel Publishing House, 1971.

Meyer, Ernest L. *"Hey! Yellowbacks!": The War Diary of a Conscientious Objector*, reprint ed. The Peace Movement in America Series, Forward by William Ellery Leonard. New York: Jerome S. Ozer, 1972.

Moore, Everett LeRoy. "Handbook of Pentecostal Denominations in the United States." M. A. thesis, Pasadena College, 1954.

National Service Board for Religious Objectors. *Statements of Religious Bodies on the Conscientious Objector*, rev. Washington, D.C.: National Service Board for Religious Objectors, 1953.
Nichol, John Thomas. *Pentecostalism*. New York: Harper and Row Publishers, 1966.
Parham, Charles F[ox]. *The Everlasting Gospel*, reprint ed. n.p., n.d.
Parham, Sarah T. *The Life of Charles F. Parham*. Joplin, Mo.: Tri-State Printing Co., 1930.
Patterson, J[ames] O[glethorpe].; Ross, German R.; and Atkins, Julia Mason. *History and Formative Years of the Church of God in Christ with Excerpts from the Life and Works of its Founder: Bishop C. H. Mason*. Memphis: Church of God in Christ Publishing House, 1969.
Paul, George H. "The Religious Frontier in Oklahoma: Dan T. Muse and the Pentecostal Holiness Church." Ph.D. dissertation, University of Oklahoma, 1965.
Paulk, Earl P. *Your Pentecostal Neighbor*. Cleveland, Tenn.: Pathway Press, 1958.
Perry, Shawn. *Words of Conscience: Religious Statements on Conscientious Objection*. Washington, D.C.: National Interreligious Service Board for Conscientious Objectors, 1980.
Peterson, H. C. and Fite, Gilbert C. *Opponents of War 1917-1918*. Madison: University of Wisconsin Press, 1957.
Piepkorn, Arthur Carl. *Profiles in Belief*, vols. 3, 4. San Francisco: Harper and Row Publishers, 1979.
Playne, Caroline E. *Society at War 1914-1916*. Boston: Houghton Mifflin Company, 1931.
Sandeen, Ernest R. *The Roots of Fundamentalism*. Chicago: University of Chicago Press, 1970.
Schlissel, Lillian, ed. *Conscience in America: A Documentary of Conscientious Objection in America, 1757-1967*. New York: E. P. Dutton Co. Inc., 1968.
Schwartz, Gary. *Sect Ideologies and Social Status*. Chicago: University of Chicago Press, 1970.
Selective Service System. *Conscientious Objection*. Special Monograph no. 11, Vol. 1. Washington, D.C.: Government Printing Office, 1950.
Smith, C. Henry. *The Story of the Mennonites*. Berne, Ind.: Mennonite Book Concern, n.d.
Smith, Timothy L. *Revivalism and Social Reform in Mid-Nineteenth-Century America*. New York: Abingdon Press, 1957.

Stark, Werner. *The Sociology of Religion: A Study of Christendom*, 5 vols., Vol 2: Sectarian Religion. New York: Fordham University Press, 1967.
Stone, James. *The Church of God of Prophecy: History and Polity*. Cleveland, Tenn.: White Wing Publishing Co., 1977.
Swomley, John M. *The Military Establishment*. Forward by Senator George McGovern. Boston: Beacon Press, 1964.
Synan, Vinson., ed. *Aspects of Pentecostal-Charismatic Origins*. Plainfield, N.J.: Logos International, 1975.
_____. *The Holiness-Pentecostal Movement in the United States*. Grand Rapids: William B. Eerdmans Publishing Company, 1971.
_____. *The Old-Time Power*. Franklin Springs, GA.: Advocate Press, 1973.
Thomas, Norman. *Is Conscience a Crime?* new ed., Foreward by Charles Chatfield. New York: Garland Publishing, Inc., 1972.
Tomlinson, Homer. *The diary of A. J. Tromlinson*. Vol. II. Queens, N.Y.: Church of God World Headquarters, 1949.
A Voice from Zion: Sermons and Addresses by the Rev. John Alexander Dowie. Vols. I, II, III, and IV, Chicago: Zion Printing and Publishing House, 1901-1902.
Waldvogel, Edith Lydia. "The 'Overcoming Life': A Study in the Reformed Evangeical Origins of Pentecostalism." Ph.D. thesis, Harvard University, 1977.
Wilson, Bryan R. *Sects and Society: A Sociological Study of Three Religious Groups in Britain*. Westport, Conn.: Greenwood Press, 1961.
Wilson, P. W. *General Evangeline Booth of the Salvation Army*. New York: Charles Scribner's Sons, 1948.
Wittlinger, Carlton O. *Quest for Piety and Obedience: The Story of the Brethren in Christ*. Nappanee, Ind.: Evangel Press, 1978.

Articles

"All Nations Now Enter Their Golden Age: Bishop Tomlinson to Visit, Reassure Rulers: 12-Day World-Flight as Prophet, Oct. 7-19." *The Church of God*, October l, 1963, pp. 1-3.
"Are You Off to the Front?" *Weekly Evangel*, September 11, 1915, p. 1.
Bartleman, Frank. "The European War." *Weekly Evangel*, July 10, 1915, p. 3.

_____. "Present Day Conditions." *Weekly Evangel*, June 5, 1915, p. 3.

_____. "What Will the Harvest Be?" *Weekly Evangel*, August 7, 1915, pp. 1-2.

Beacham, Paul F. "Light on the Subject." *Pentecostal Holiness Advocate*, November 27, 1952, n.p.

Bell, E. N. "Destroy This Tract." *Christian Evangel*, August 24, 1918, p. 4.

_____. "The League of Nations." *Christian Evangel*, March 8, 1919, p. 2.

_____. "Preachers Warned." *Weekly Evangel*, January 5, 1918, p. 4.

_____. "Questions and Answers." *Christian Evangel*, October 19, 1918, p. 5.

_____. "Questions and Answers." *Weekly Evangel*, January 26, 1918, p. 9.

_____. "A Tremendous Day is To-Day." *Weekly Evangel*, February 23, 1918, pp. 6-7.

"Blood Against Blood. Should Christians Go to War?" *Weekly Evangel*, July 10, 1915, p. 3.

Boddy, J. T. "The Prince of Peace." *Pentecostal Evangel*, December 25, 1920, p. 1.

"Books For You to Read." *Pentecostal Evangel*, August 2, 1924, p. 16.

Booth-Clibborn, S. H. "The Christian and War. Is it Too Late?" *Weekly Evangel*, April 28, 1917, p. 5.

"Candidate for President of U.S.A., 1964: Bishop Tomlinson's Program Gains Ground" *The Church of God*, October 15, 1963, pp. 1, 3-4.

Cerillo, Augustus. "Moving Up: Some Consequences of the New A/G Social Status." *Agora 1* (Winter 1978): 8-11.

"Compulsory Military Service: An English Conscientious Movement." *Mennonite Quarterly Review* LIII (July 1979):219-234.

Dayton, Donald W. and Dayton, Lucille S. "An Historical Survey of Attitudes Toward War and Peace Within the American Holiness Movement." Winona Lake, Ind., 1973. (Typewritten.)

Dayton, Donald W. and Lucille Sider Dayton. "An Historical Survey of Attitudes Toward War and Peace Within the American Holiness Movement," in *Perfect Love and War: A Dialogue on Christian Holiness and the Issues of War and Peace*. (Nappanee, In.: 1974) pp. 132-152.

Dayton, Donald W. "Theological Roots of Pentecostalism." *Journal of the Society for Pentecostal Studies* 2 (Spring 1980):3-21.

"The Death Penalty." *Pentecostal Evangel*, January 24, 1960, p.4.

Bibliography 131

Dempster, Murray W. "Peacetime Draft Registration and Pentecostal Moral Conscience." *Agora 3* (Spring 1980):2-3.

"Editorial." *Redemption Tidings*, November 15, 1957, pp. 2-3.

Flower, J. Roswell. "The Plight of the Christian in the Present World War." *Pentecostal Evangel*, June 12, 1943, pp. 6-7.

_____. "The Plight of the Conscientious Objector in the Present World Conflict." *Pentecostal Evangel,* July 3, 1943, pp. 2-3.

F[lower], J[oseph] R[oswell]. "Prophetic War Horses Sent Out." *The Christian Evangel*, August 29, 1914, p. 1.

_____. "Should Christians Go to War?" *The Christian Evangel*, January 16, 1915, p. 2.

Frodsham, Stanley H. "Our Heavenly Citizenship." *Word and Witness*, October 1915, p. 3.

Galmond, Mary. "Testimony and Peophecy." *The Apostolic Faith*, October 1906, p. 2.

Gee, Donald. "Conscientious Objection." *Pentecostal Evangel*, May 4, 1940, p. 4, November 8, 1930, pp. 6-7, Evangel, November 15, 1930, pp. 2-3.

"Government to Investigate Case of Rev. Wm. Reid." *Sacramento Bee*, 22 December 1917, pp. 1, 4.

Hollenweger, Walter, J. "Black Pentecostal Concept." *Concept 30* (June 1970).

"Is European War Justifiable?" *The Christian Evangel*, December 12, 1914, pp. 1, 3.

Kindersley, Major Guy M. "Can Peace Come From Such Seed?" *Pentecostal Evangel*, May 15, 1920, p. 10.

"Kingdom of God Comes, 12:00 Noon July 4th: Righteousness, Peace on Earth as in Heaven." *The Church of God*, July 1, 1964, pp. 1-2.

Klippenstein, Lawrence. "Exercising a Free Conscience: The Conscientious Objectors of the Soviet Union and the German Democratic Republic." *Religion in Communist Lands*, Vol. 13, No. 3, Winter, 1985, pp. 284-285.

Lebeck, Albert J. "Will the Present Day Merging Lead to the Mark of the Beast?" *Pentecostal Evangel*, June 6, 1931, pp. 4-5.

"Light on the Present Crisis." *Weekly Evangel*, July 1, 1916, pp. 6-7, 9.

"Loyalty Bonds." *Christian Evangel,* June 1, 1918, p. 8.

McAlister, James. "Startling Signs of the Times." Pentecostal Evangel, July 10, 1920, n.p.

McCafferty, Burt. "Should Christians Go to War?" *The Christian Evangel*, January 16, 1915, p. 1.

McPherson, Warren F. "Military Service Policy Restudied by Assemblies." n.p., n.d., n.p.

Moorhead, Max Wood. "The Perils of Bolshevism at Home and Abroad." *Pentecostal Evangel*, February 7, 1920, n.p.

"New Bylaws on Military Service Adopted by General Council." *Pentecostal Evangel*, October 8, 1967, n.p.

"News Release." *The Church of God* (News Release Issue), October 15, 1963, p. l.

"Pacifist Pastor Gets 15 Years." *Boston Globe*, 22 March 1918, p. 1, col. 3, p. 5 col. 6.

Panton, D. M. "Democracy and the End." *Weekly Evangel*, April 17, 1915, p. l.

Paul, Ernest A. "The Great War Thru the Lens of Prophecy." *The Pentecostal Herald*, March 1917, p. 1.

Pierce, Christine K. "Birth Throes." *Pentecostal Evangel*, February 4, 1922, pp. 1-2.

"The Pentecostal Movement and the Conscription Law." *Weekly Evangel*, August 4, 1917, pp. 6-7.

"The Pentecostal Movement and the Conscription Law." *Weekly Evangel*, January 5, 1918, p. 5.

"Pentecostal Saints Opposed to War." *Weekly Evangel*, June 19, 1915, p. 1.

Polman, G. R. "A. A. Boddy Goes to the Front." *Weekly Evangel*, June 19, 1915, p. 1.

"Questions Answered." *The Apostolic Faith*, October to January 1908, p. 2.

Richey, Raymond T. "Amongst the Soldier Boys." *Weekly Evangel*, February 16, 1918, p. 7.

Rotzel, H[arold] L. "Vermont's Sedition Trial," *New York Evening Post*, 4 February 1918, p. 9, col. 1-6.

"Russia Preparing for War." *Pentecostal Evangel*, July 26, 1924, p. 7.

"Sacramento Pastor Jailed on Charge of Sedition." *Sacramento Bee*, 21 December 1917.

Schell, William G. "The Daily Lives of the Early Christians." *Weekly Evangel*, October 30, 1915, p. 1.

_____. The Daily Lives of the Early Christians." *Weekly Evangel*, November 6, 1915, p. 1.

"Shout! Pray On! We're Gaining Ground: Hallelu! Now, Every Creature." *The Church of God*, November 15, 1964, pp. 1-2.

Sisler, George T. "War 'Profits.'" *Weekly Evangel*, April 19, 1916, p. 7.

"The Sixth Commandment." *At Ease*, Summer, n.d., pp. 7-11.

"Testimony Given in Sedition Case." *Christian Science Monitor*, 10 January 1918, p. 6.
"War! War!! War!!!" *The Christian Evangel*, August 15, 1914, p.1.
Warner, Wayne E. "The St. Louis Era." *Heritage*, Fall 1981, pp. 1-2.
Welch, J. W. "An Explanation." *Weekly Evangel*, May 19, 1917, p. 8.
Williams, Ernest S. "The Conscientious Objector." *Pentecostal Evangel*, June 15, 1940, pp. 4-5.
_____. "Our Duty as Christian Citizens." *Pentecostal Evangel*, November 28, 1936, pp. 1, 3.
_____. "Questions and Answers." *Pentecostal Evangel*, July 27, 1940, p. 5.
_____. "Your Questions." *Pentecostal Evangel*, February 12, 1961, p. 11.
_____. "Your Questions." *Pentecostal Evangel*, February 13, 1966, p. 11.
Ytterock, Dave. "Probing Our Moral Identity." *Agora 1* (Fall 1977): p. 6-9.

Pamphlets

The Articles of Faith: The Church of God of the Apostolic Faith Inc. Tulsa, Okla.: n.p., 1951.
Bartleman, Frank. *Christian Citizenship*. Los Angeles: By the Author, n.d.
_____. *War and the Christian*. Los Angeles: By the Author, n.d.
Booth-Clibborn, William E. *A Call to Dust and Ashes*. St. Paul, Minn.: By the Author, n.d.
The Case of the Christian Pacifists at Los Angeles, Cal. New York: National Civil Liberties Bureau, 1918.
Church News Service: A Public Information Service of the National Association of Evangelicals, "National Association of Evangelicals States Position on Civil Disobedience." February 1, 1966.
Constitution and By-Laws: The Filipino Assemblies of the First-born, Incorporated. Delano, Calif.: n.p., 1975.
Discipline of the Congregational Holiness Church. n.p., 1966.
General Constitution and By-Laws of the Pentecostal Church of God of America. Joplin, Mo.: n.p., 1975.
Kasdorf, George. *The Christian--and War!* Springfield, Mo.: Artcraft Gospell Press, n.d.
A Patriotic Harlot. n.p., n.d.

Letters

C[unningham], R[obert] C. to Mrs. Clarence Zeilke, February 3, 1967.
_____. to Rebecca Francis, June 25, 1971.
_____. to W[illiam] Suttles, September 8, 1972.
Francis, Rebecca. to Editor of the Pentecostal Evangel, June 16, 1971.
F[rodsham], S[tanley] H. to Leslie Wattenburger, November 26, 1941.
Peterson, Paul B. to Noel Perkin, September 21, 1928.
_____. to Noel Perkin, June 13, 1929.
_____. to Noel Perkin, July 12, 1929.
Wattenburger, Leslie C. to Editor of the Pentecostal Evangel, November 24, 1941.
Webb, Bert. to Bob Cunningham, May 31, 1961.
_____. to Bob Cunningham, July 17, 1961.

Minutes

Free Methodist Church, Annual Minutes. Chicago: Free Methodist Publishing House, 1914, 1916, 1917.
General Council of the Assemblies of God, Combined Minutes. Springfield, Mo.: Gospel Publishing House, 1918.
General Council of the Assemblies of God, Constitution and Bylaws. Springfield, Mo.: Gospel Publishing House, 1927, 1929, 1930, 1931, 1932, 1935, 1937, 1939, 1941, 1943, 1945, 1951, 1953, 1957, 1959, 1965, 1967.
General Council of the Assemblies of God, Combined Minutes. St. Louis, Mo.: Gospel Publishing House, 1914, 1916, 1917.
Resolutions Processed for Presentation to the 39th General Council Convening in St. Louis, Missouri August 20-25, 1981. n.p., n.d.

Interviews

Menzies, William. Springfield, Mo. Phone Interview, November 1980.
O'Guin, Carl. Madison, Ill. Phone Interview, 16 January 1982.
Waugh, Chaplain Earl. Assemblies of God Headquarters, Springfield, Mo. Interview, 3 September 1981.

NAME INDEX

A

Abrams, Ray H., 2, 89
Anderson, Robert Mapes, 51, 91

B

Baker, David, 51
Barkley, Colonel David, 67n.
Bartleman, Frank, 54-58, 76
Bell, Endorus N., 74-76, 94n., 114
Biffle, Silas, 103
Boddy, Alexander A., 71, 84, 86
Booth, General William, 42, 44
Booth-Clibborn, Arthur Sydney, 40-42, 47-48, 56, 61, 68n., 86
Booth-Clibborn, Catherine (Katie), 42, 47-48
Bush, Howard, 120n.

C

Campbell, Alexander, 14, 20n.
Cantell, Margaret, 56
Carter, Howard, 64, 101, 112, 120n.
Carter, John, 101, 112
Cerillo, Augustus, 112
Chafee, Zechariah, 104n.
Champion, Richard, 114
Clibborn, see also Booth-Clibborn.
Clibborn, John, 67n.
Colburn, Ralph, 115
Constantine, 43
Craig, W. S., 9

Cummings, Howard, 120n.
Curry, A. Stauffer, 18n.

D

Darby, John Nelson, 3
Darms, Anton, 50
Dayton, Donald, 3, 17n.
Dayton, Lucille S[ider], 17n.
DeGroot, Alfred T., 20n.
Dempster, Murray W., 117, 121n.
Dieter, Melvin, 4
Dresser, Amos, 5-6

E

Elijah, the Restorer, 38, 48-49; see Dowie, J. A..
Ellenberg, Chaplain R., 119n.
Ewert, Jacob G., 105n.

F

Faupel, David W., 22
Fenelon, 5
Flower, Joseph, 103, 105n.
Foster, Atwood, 112

G

Gerhart, J. L., 120n.
Groves, Anthony Norris, 19n.
Guyon, Madame, 5

H

Hall, Percy Francis, 19n.
Harrison, John Irvine, 110
Harrup, O. B., 120n.

Hollenweger, Walter J., 27, 33, 85, 121n.
Howe, Julia Ward, 2

J
Jamison, S. A., 90, 96n.
Jeffreys, George, 120n.
John the Baptist, 38
Jones, Charles, 10

K
Kellogg, Major, 102
Kercher, Leon G., 119n.
Kolenda, Daniel P., 120n.

L
Lang, George Henry, 20n.
Lowe, Thomas, 67n.
Lynch, Lycurgus Reuben, 81-83

M
Mason, Charles H., 26, jailed, 100
McCafferty, William Burton, 87-88, 95n.
McIntire, Carl, 111
McKinley, President, 40
McPherson, Warren F., 115-116
McWhirter, James 112, 119n.
Mellor, Ernest T., 101
Menzies, William, 106, 119n.
Meyer, Ernest, 102
Moody, Dwight L., 13

N
Neve, J. L., 105

O
O'Guin, Carl, 90, 103

P
Palmer, Phoebe, 4
Parham, Charles Fox, 51, 53-54
Penn, William, 67n.
Peterson, Bartlett, 120n.
Pierson, 103
Polhill, Cecil, 84-86
Polman, G. R., 87

R
Reid, William, 99-100
Restorer, Elijah 38; see Dowie, J. A..
Richardson, Wilfred, 101
Richey, Raymond T., 88, 90
Robbins, Roger, 66n.
Robeck, Cecil Mel, 66n.
Robertson, William H., 120n.
Romack, Rolland, 52
Roosevelt, President, 48

S
Scroggie, W. Graham, 86
Shelhamer, E. E., 9
Simpson, A. B., 11
Smales, Clarence P., 110
Smith, Hannah Whitall, 18n.
Smith, Robert Pearsall, 18n.
Smith, Timothy, 2
Studd, C. T., 85
Suttles, William, 117

T

Thistlethwaites, 51
Tomlison, Ambrose Jessup, 90-92; disloyalty, 92; investigated, 100
Tomlison, Homer, 91, 94; Cadet Corps, 92; Tanks Corps, 92
Tomlison, Milton, 92
Torrey, Reuben, 3

W

Waldron, Clarence H., 13, 98-99, 104n.

Warner, Daniel, 10
Washington, George; vision, 52
Wattenburger, Leslie C., 112-113
Way, Rev. Robert R., 115
Williams, Ernest S., 77-78, 80-81, 95n., 114
Wilson, Bryan R., 108
Wilson, Dwight J., 66
Wilson, President, 88
Wilson, Robert, 18n.

Y

Ytterock, Dave, 117

INDEX OF RELIGIOUS DENOMINATIONS AND RELIGIOUS MOVEMENTS

A

Anabaptists, 10, 83
Anglican Church, 85
Apostolic Church (South Wales), 32
Apostolic Faith, 105n.
Apostolic Gospel Church of Jesus Christ, 28
Assemblies of God, 1, 24-25, 105n., 110-12, 114-17; Servicemen's Department, 109
Assemblies of the Lord Jesus Christ, 28
Associated Brotherhood of Christians, 28

B

Baptist, 98
Bible Holiness Movement, 12
Brethren in Christ, 11

C

Calvary Pentecostal Church, 25, 35n.
Christ Faith Mission, 25, 35n.
Christ's Sanctified Holy Church (West Columbia, S.C.), 12
Christian Assembly, 106n.
Christian Catholic Church, 50
Christian Church of North America, 25
Church in Jesus Name, 105n.

Church of God, 106n.
Church of God (1957 Reformation), 26
Church of God (1957 reformation, Cleveland), 35n.
Church of God (Anderson, Indiana), 10
Church of God (Apostolic) (Black Holiness), 28
Church of God (Apostolic, 1901), 27
Church of God (Cleveland) 1, 26, 90-92, 100, 110
Church of God (Guthrie, Oklahoma), 12
Church of God (Huntsville, Al.), 90, 93
Church of God (Mountain Assembly), 26
Church of God (original), 35n., 91
Church of God (Queens, N.Y.), 92
Church of God (Winebrennerian), 10
Church of God in Christ (black), 1, 26 100, 104n., 105n.
Church of the Lord Jesus Christ of the Apostolic Faith, 27
Church of the Nazarene, 7
Churches of God (Independent Holiness People), 12
Churches of God of the Original Mountain Assembly, 26, 35n.
Community Full Gospel Church, 105n.
Congregational Holiness Church, 26

D

Disciples of Christ, 14

E

Elim Foursquare Gospel Church, 32, 112, 120n.
Emmanuel Association, 10
Emmanuel Holiness Church, 26, 35n.
Evangelical, 111, 120n., 123
Evangelical Mennonite, 18

F

Faith Tabernacle, 105n.
Filipino Assemblies of the First-Born, 25, 35n.
Fire Baptized Holiness Church, 12, 19, 26
First Ukranian Evangelical Pentecostal Assembly, 105n.
Friends, Reconstruction Unit, 105n., see also Quakers.

G

Gospel Mission Corps, 12, 19

H

Holiness Christian Church of the United States, 12, 19
Holiness Church at Camp Creek, 90-91
Holiness Movement, 1-2, 10-11
Holiness Pentecostal Denominations, 26

Index of Religious Denominations/Movements

K
Keswick, 22, 86
Keswick Pentecostal Denominations, 25

L
Latin-American Council of the Pentecostal Churches, 25

M
Mennonites, 10-11, 99
Mt. Sinai Holy Church of America, Incorporated, 29

N
National Association of Evangelicals, 109, 111-112, 114-115
Negro Church of God, 14

O
Olzabal Latin-American Council of Churches, 25, 35n.
Oneness Pentecostal Denominations, 28
Open Bible Standard, 105n.
Open Brethren, 13
Original Church of God, 26

P
Pentecostal, 105n.
Pentecostal Assemblies of God, 105n.
Pentecostal Assemblies of the World, 28, 99
Pentecostal Church of God of America, 35n.
Pentecostal Fire Baptized Holiness Church, 26, 35n.
Pentecostal Holiness Church, 1, 26, 110
Pentecostal Missionary Union, 84
Philadelphia Church, 105n.
Pietism, 4
Pilgrim Holiness Church, 10
Plymouth Brethren, 13
Prophecy Conference Movement, 3

Q
Quakers, 10, 18, 33, 41-42, 51, 54, 67-68n., 91, 105n.

R
Reformed Evangelical, 1, 13

S
Southern Baptist, Southern Seminary, 94
Swedish Pentecostals, 121n.
Swiss Pentecostal Mission, 33
Swiss Pentecostal Movement, 33

T
Triumph Church, 27

W
Wesleyan Methodists, 7

Y
Y.M.C.A., 88-89

SUBJECT INDEX

A
All Saints, Suderland, 85
Ambulance corps, 49
American Indians, 58
Anglo-Boer War, 67n.
Azusa Street, 54

B
Battle Hymn, 2
Biblical literalism, 20
Blood Against Blood, 51
Boy Scouts movement, 92
Britain, see England.
British, see England.
British Israelism, 119n.
Broadway Tabernacle, N.Y. 79

C
Cambridge Seven, 85
Camp Sherman, 89
Canada, 33
Capital punishment, 45
Central Bible Institute, 81, 110
Chaplaincy, 109-114
Citizenship, 55, 59, 78, 86-7
Civil defense shelters, 114
Civil disobedience, 76, 115, 120n.
Civil War, 2, 13
Civilian Public Service Camps, 103
Combatant, 117
Compulsory military training, 119n.
Conscientious objection 64, 89, 101-2, 105n., 108, 113, 115, 117
Cultural conformity, 112
Culver Military Academy, 92

D
Dartmoor Prison, 65, 101
Department of Justice, investigation, 91
Depression Era, 78

E
Edinburgh, 60; University, 39
Education, 75
England, 1, 33, 56-57, 60, 64, 84-86, 97, 101, 108, 114
Eschatology, vii, 43-45, 51-52, 60, 75; Great Tribulation, 93; Kingdom, 78; Postmillenial, 2; Return of Christ, 113; British Israelism, 119n.
Espionage Act, 58, 74, 98; see also sedition act.
Ethical attitudes, 117
Executioners, 82
Expeditionary Forces, Chaplain, 87

F
Fanaticism, 78
Farm colony, 101
Flag, see government.
Fort Leavenworth, 102

Subject Index

G

Georgia Penitentiary, 99
German prisoners, 86
German sympathizer, 100
Germany, 33, 56-57, 121n.
G. I. Bill, 110
Government, 75, 82; Department of Justice investigation, 91; flag, 75; legitimacy, 31; loyalty to, 31, 74, 117; magistrates 82; politics, 55; Theocratic Party, 93
Great Britain, see England.
Great Tribulation, see eschatology.

H

H-Bomb, 114
Harringay, 61
Healing Ministry, 44
Holy Rollers, 15

I

Individual conscience, 80
Italy, 113

J

Jail, 74; see also prison.

K

Kingdom, see eschatology.

L

Legitimacy, see government.
Liberty Bonds, 75, 94
Loyalty Bonds, 76
Loyalty; see government.
Lusitania, 58

M

Magistrates, 82
Medical, service, 65; duty, 48
Military; Ambulance Corps, 49; Camp Sherman, 89; chaplaincy, 109-114; combatant, 117; compulsory military training, 119; see also, conscientious objector; Fort Leavenworth, 102; G. I. Bill, 110; medical service 65; ministerial exemption 109; see also, noncombatant.
Ministerial exemption, 109
Missions, opposed to war spirit, vii, 38; Bartleman, 55; Booth-Clibborns, 43-45; Parham, 54;
Missionaries, Booth-Clibborns, 42; to servicemen, see Raymond T. Richey.
Munitions, 83
Murder, 80, 113-114

N

Nationalism, 52-53, 59, 78; see also patriotism.
New Covenant, 82
New Testament, 82
Noachian Covenant, 82
Noncombatant, 32, 63, 80, 83-84, 101, 103-105n., 109, 113, 117

O

Old Testament, 82; Naochian Covenant, 82; Sixth Commandment, 116

P

Patriotism, 52-53, 55, 59, 62, 75, 78, 120n.; see also nationalism.
Perfectionism, 4
Policemen, 82
Politics, see government.
Postmillenial, see eschatology.
Prince of Peace, 60
Prison; Jail, 74; Dartmoor Prison, 65, 101; Fort Leavenworth, 102; Georgia Penitentiary, 99; Wakefield Prison, 101; Wormwood Scrubbs Prison, London, 65, 101
Professionalized clergy, 108-109; ministerial exemption to draft, 109; rail discounts, 108

R

Rail discounts, 108
Red Cross, 75
Religious entrepreneur, 39
Religious liberty, 113
Restorationism, 38
Return of Christ, see eschatology.
Reveille, 109, 111
Revivalism, 4
Russia, 33, 56
Russian Pentecostals, 33
Russio-Japanese War, 49

S

Scripture, vii
Sect, 108
Sedition Act, 58, 74, 76, 98; see also Espionage Act.
Sermon on the Mount, vii, 33, 71
Servicemen's representative, 115
Sixth Commandment, 116
Social mobility, vii
Social status, 1, 75, 85, 108; status mobility, 39
Soviet, see Russia.
Spanish-American War, 40
Suicide, 116
Sydney, Australia, 39

T

Tax; World Peace Tax Fund, 117
Theocratic Party, 93
Treason, 74
Treveca College, 99

W

Wakefield Prison, 101
Welch Revival, 60
Westfield Academy, 91
World Peace Tax Fund, 117
World War I, 97; Espionage Act; 58, 74, 98; Sedition Act, 58, 74, 76, 98; conscientious objection, 101
World War II, 51, 64, 79, 84-85, 88-89, 91, 97, 103, 108-12
Wormwood Scrubbs Prison, London, 65, 101

Z

Zion, Il., 39

www.ingramcontent.com/pod-product-compliance
Lightning Source LLC
Chambersburg PA
CBHW062040220426
43662CB00010B/1588